RECIPES FROM A
SOUTHERN RESTAURANT

Classics

To Jan

Happy cookin !

ISBN-10: 1456321757
EAN-13: 9781456321758

We dedicate this book to the farmers and fishermen who enable our cooking.

Wadmalaw Island Farmer, Celeste Albers

low country

Table of Contents

Powermove = ♥ + food

Our Restaurant

The Glass Onion restaurant came to be in March 2008 through the combined efforts of myself (Sarah O'Kelley) and my two business partners, Charles Vincent and Chris Stewart. Located in Charleston, South Carolina, we pride ourselves on serving delicious Southern food inspired by local, all-natural ingredients. Here we offer up some of our staple recipes that truly embody the spirit of the Glass Onion.

Our daily menu can be found at www.ilovetheglassonion.com, along with further information about the restaurant.

Our Thanks

I am filled with undying gratitude to the many people who have made the Glass Onion restaurant – and now this cookbook – possible. Our ever-supportive families and friends appreciated our food from day one and pushed us onward and upward. Thank you!

Appreciation related specifically to the publication of *Glass Onion Classics* must begin with gratitude for my business partner, Chris Stewart, and our co-founding partner, Charles Vincent.

Next, I must give handfuls of thanks to my collaborators on this book. *Glass Onion Classics* owes much of its readability and beauty to these folks.

Suzanne Kelly Stewart proved to be a copy editing genius, never tiring of finding the clearest explanation in regard to cooking technique. And she gave me a whole new relationship with the comma!

Zachary Trefsger poured his heart and soul into the illustrations you find in this book. He truly captured the spirit of our food and philosophy.

Suzanne Jones Hughston enhanced my farm photography with her superior editing ability and expert eye for a balanced portrait.

John Smoak nailed our cover with his killer photographic instinct. He took my very loose idea and created an image that syncs all of our GO sensibilities together.

Craig McAdams also added to the cover with his food styling, proving himself to truly be the "Egg Man."

Peter Frank Edwards proved his artistic excellence and incredible patience in capturing the genuine personalities of all three of us owners with his lens.

On a personal note, I must thank my grandmother, Sarah Hughston, and my mother, Louise O'Kelley, for giving me the foundation from which all my creative ability comes. And I must undeniably thank Jeff Hoekman for his unflagging enthusiasm for tasting dish upon dish even when they lacked perfection!

Last but very far from least, I thank our staff at the restaurant who gave me the peace of mind to step away long enough to complete this project. Namely, I give supreme thanks to Sara Oakes, the best general manager in all the land!

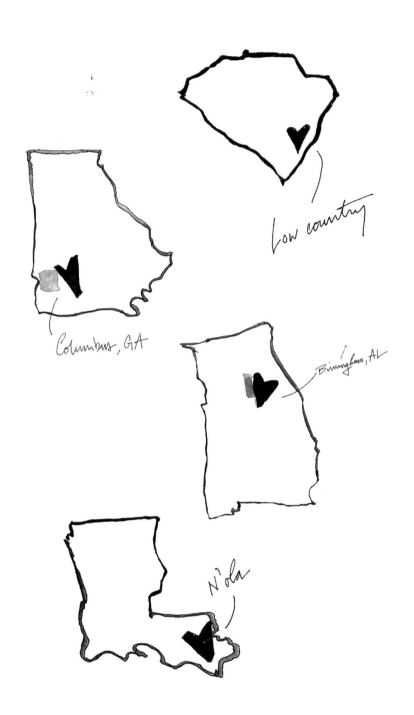

Low country

Columbus, GA

Birmingham, AL

N'ola

Our Philosophy

Somewhere in the midst of our busy, harried lives, the simple, everyday pleasure of a delicious meal has lost its way. At the Glass Onion, we beg to differ. We believe that a day is not complete without a meal that satisfies the soul.

Charles, Chris, and I all grew up with food as a focal point in our lives and want to remind customers of the joy brought about by perfectly fried chicken, hearty gumbo, crisp homemade pickles, and soft, buttery cookies. Furthermore, we want to nurture the reconnection with the origin of this food.

We take pride in supporting local farmers and fishermen by using as many local, all-natural ingredients as possible. Their food frankly tastes better. But knowing the face of the person who raised the chickens, caught the shrimp, and harvested the vegetables also makes the entire experience profoundly richer.

So here we offer up some of our Glass Onion classics that showcase the bounty of the Lowcountry and our roots in Alabama, Louisiana, and Georgia. And we also offer up some of the stories behind this food, introducing you to our farmers, fishermen, and other folks who inspire the Glass Onion. As you try out these recipes, we encourage you to meet *your* local farmers and fishermen and discover our fundamental truth – local food tastes better!

Thanks for eating!

Sarah, Charles, and Chris

Chris Stewart, Charles Vincent, Sarah O'Kelley

ABOUT US

Sarah O'Kelley
I honestly believe that life just doesn't get any better than a tomato sandwich on white bread with plenty of Duke's mayonnaise. My dark secret happens to be that during my childhood in Georgia, I actually knew nothing but Hellman's. Yet, somehow I still managed to find a career in food. A winding path via kitchens and keyboards brought jobs with Emeril and various publications in New Orleans and Charleston. This and my gift for gab enables my non-stop talk about all food topics. So, I will be happy to explain every nuance of the Glass Onion to any willing person, but don't get me started on mayonnaise.

Charles Vincent
Charles grew up in New Orleans, Louisiana and cut his teeth on trout amandine and barbecue shrimp. That early palate workout led to a life centered on the kitchen. From Emeril's Delmonico in New Orleans to FIG here in Charleston, Charles honed his culinary skills and appetite for all good food. While fine dining certainly falls within that realm, he really idealizes the genuine fare of his favorite old New Orleans haunts – namely po boys. Thanks to his homesickness for honest-to-goodness po boys on legitimate po boy bread, you will find the real deal at the Glass Onion.

Chris Stewart
As an eighth-generation Alabama native, Chris hails from a rich tradition of Southern eating and cooking. Growing up in Birmingham, his earliest memories include boiled green peanuts, vegetables straight

out of the garden, and his Momma's country fried steak. Summers spent at his grandparents' house in Savannah eventually drew him to Charleston where he attended Johnson and Wales University. Upon graduation, he furthered his passion in kitchens like SNOB before becoming the sous chef at FIG. But really it all goes back to that country fried steak. Chris sets out to make his Momma proud by occasionally serving his version at the Glass Onion.

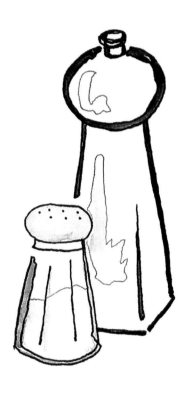

Thoughts on Cooking

Before you jump into *Glass Onion Classics*, we would like to share a few general ideas on the subject of cooking, specifically from our cookbook.

First, it is definitely a cookbook that is meant to be put to good use. While we would love for you to display it on your coffee table, we also fully intend for you to cook your way through these GO staples. With this in mind, we tested all of the recipes in a home kitchen, with an electric stove, using as few gadgets as possible.

You see, we believe that it is possible to produce absolutely delicious food in a modest environment. There are a few tricks of the trade we thought to share, usually as a postscript at the bottom of the recipe. But ultimately, we believe that the quality of the food lies in the ingredients, not the tools.

That said, we try not call for any crazily esoteric ingredients. This is simply not our style. You should be able to complete most of your grocery list at an ordinary grocery store. For special ingredients like whole spices, you might try visiting a health food store or gourmet shop. And for regional ingredients like crawfish and andouille sausage, we have included a list of sources (see page XXV).

If you are an adventurous cook on a mission for authenticity, please use this sourcing page to your heart's content. But in case you are short on time or money, we try to provide alternatives. We encourage you to use this cookbook as a guide, not a rule book.

That said, we also hope that you cook to your own taste. If you know that your palate is sensitive to salt or heat, follow your inner cues. We like well-seasoned food, but you might prefer less. Or you very well might prefer more!

Most of all, we want you to enter your kitchen with confidence. Don't be afraid to crank up the heat when you need a good sear. And certainly don't be afraid to tackle a task for the first time – like making pie dough from scratch!

Hopefully, as you cook through *Glass Onion Classics*, you will come to know yourself better as a cook, trusting your own best judgement, and most of all, enjoying the time spent preparing good food.

Sourcing

Anson Mills, South Carolina – www.ansonmills.com
*For grits, peas, cornmeal, and many more artisanal grains.

Allan Benton, Tennessee – www.bentonshams.com
*For handcrafted bacon and country hams.

Poche's, Louisiana – www.pochesmarket.com
*For any of your Cajun needs – andouille sausage, boudin, crawfish, etc. They make all of their own sausages!

The Cajun Connection, Louisiana – www.cajunconnection.com
*For more Louisiana products – specifically, Zatarain's Creole Mustard, Crystal Hot Sauce, and Bulliard's Hot Sauce.

P.S. A short note on seasoning...

We firmly believe in using kosher salt and freshly ground pepper. Kosher salt can be found in your everyday grocery, as can black peppercorns.

If you happen to be cooking a great deal in one day, you might grind a handful of peppercorns in a coffee grinder to save time. To clean the grinder before and after grinding the pepper, simply grind an absorbent, neutral-tasting cracker or cereal in the grinder. Then wipe out the residue. This should save your coffee from tasting like pepper, and your pepper from tasting like coffee!

And as far as hot sauces, our favorites are Crystal, Bulliard's, and Tabasco. We prefer Crystal and Bulliard's for use in recipes, as they don't have the overwhelming heat and very specific flavor of Tabasco. However, it is always nice to have Tabasco on the table, and it is quite easy to find in grocery stores everywhere. Just be aware that it does pack more of a spicy punch if you are using it in recipes.

And lastly, we strongly recommend that you use fresh garlic as opposed to the jarred, pre-minced variety. If you happen to hate mincing garlic, then consider treating yourself to the nifty tool known as the Microplane grater. The fine-toothed Microplane will yield "minced" garlic in seconds!

CHAPTER 1

Kitchen Basics

Really Good Chicken Stock

Housemade stock is a staple at the GO and really elevates dishes to another level. Granted, making it is a time-consuming process, but it is actually pretty simple and will make your house smell like the coziest place on earth. Besides, what could be more rewarding on a cold winter weekend than filling your freezer with stock!

4½ pounds chicken bones, such as necks or backs
2 cups roughly chopped onion (about 1 medium onion)
2 cups peeled, roughly chopped carrots
    (about 2 medium carrots)
2 cups roughly chopped celery
    (about 6 medium stalks)
1 head of garlic, pointy top cut off
About 20 sprigs of fresh thyme
1 bay leaf
2 tablespoons black peppercorns

Place chicken bones in a large pot (preferably 8-quart stockpot) and cover with cold water. Quickly bring to a boil over high heat. Remove from the heat and strain off the water, using a colander.

Place the chicken bones back in the pot and cover, filling pot with 5 quarts cold water. Bring to a boil, skimming off fat/foam with a ladle. Reduce to a simmer and cook for 3 hours. Add onions, carrots, celery, garlic, thyme, bay leaf, and peppercorns; simmer for 3 more hours. During simmering, add water as necessary to maintain the same level in the pot.

Strain stock into another large pot or container. Allow to cool and refrigerate or freeze in appropriate containers.

YIELD: 4 to 5 quarts (depending on the size of your pot)

P.S. As already stated, much of this recipe depends on what size pot you happen to have in your home kitchen. This was tested in an 8-quart pot and yielded about 5 quarts of stock. However, the same recipe can be accomplished in a slightly smaller pot. Your yield will be less, and the stock will be more concentrated.

Tartar Sauce

My partner Charles and I both grew up with home-made tartar sauce as a fixture. His father, Bland, made his with plenty of capers and dill. The cook at my grandmother's beach house, Ruth, made hers with sliced green olives. For the GO, we decided to combine both of these ideas for the best tartar sauce ever! I guarantee you will never go back to the jarred stuff!

Read Ruth's story on page 161.

1 cup mayonnaise
1 tablespoon capers
3 tablespoons sweet pickle relish
3 tablespoons pureed olives
2 teaspoons red wine vinegar
1 teaspoon hot sauce
1 teaspoon Worcestershire sauce
1½ teaspoons dried dill
Pinch of cayenne

Combine all ingredients in a medium bowl; stir thoroughly with a rubber spatula until well combined.

YIELD: About 1½ cups – enough to go with Mustard Fried Catfish (see page 48)

Cocktail Sauce

Some might balk at making their own cocktail sauce. After all, it's so straightforward, why not just pick some up at the grocery? Well, after spending many a childhood afternoon at Rose Hill Oyster Bar with my father, I beg to differ. Papa taught me the secret to great cocktail sauce, and I am happy to share. The key ingredient is the horseradish. Under no circumstances should you buy the creamy, jarred stuff. In the refrigerator section of your grocery (maybe in the deli), you should be able to find the "prepared" horseradish, which really possesses much more flavor!

1 cup ketchup
$^1/_3$ cup prepared horseradish
1 ½ tablespoons Worcestershire sauce
1 tablespoon fresh lemon juice
1 teaspoon hot sauce

Combine all ingredients in a medium bowl; whisk until incorporated.

YIELD: About 1 ½ cups

Red Remoulade

Remoulade is a classic French mayonnaise-based sauce. And like many French culinary traditions, it is a staple in the cuisine of south Louisiana. You might toss peeled, boiled shrimp in it for the famed shrimp remoulade salad found on many New Orleans menus. Or you might use it simply as a dipping sauce for our Peel-n-Eat Boiled Shrimp (see recipe on page 35). At the GO, we use it on many plates – even as a garnish for fried green tomatoes.

1 cup mayonnaise
¼ cup ketchup
2 tablespoons Creole mustard, or other whole grain mustard
2 tablespoons prepared horseradish
½ teaspoon kosher salt
½ teaspoon freshly ground black pepper
¹/₈ teaspoon cayenne
Splash of hot sauce

Combine all ingredients in a medium bowl; whisk until well combined.

YIELD: About 1½ cups (enough to dress 1 pound of peeled, boiled shrimp)

P.S. You can leave out the ketchup, making it "white remoulade" – a similarly tasty sauce!

House Vinaigrette

This is really a classic French vinaigrette, and that's all nice lettuce needs. Here at the restaurant, we use a hydroponic Bibb lettuce from Wes at Kurios Farms, located in nearby Moncks Corner. When available, we also use his black cherry tomatoes and gorgeous cucumbers.

Read Wes's story on page 13.

¼ cup red wine vinegar
1 tablespoon Creole
    mustard, or other
    whole grain mustard
2 teaspoons minced garlic
    (about 2 medium garlic
    cloves)
2 teaspoons minced
    shallot (about ½
    medium shallot)
1½ teaspoons fresh
    lemon juice
¾ cup vegetable oil
¹/₃ cup extra-virgin olive oil
2 teaspoons kosher salt
2 teaspoons freshly ground
    black pepper

Row upon row of Bibb lettuce at Kurios Farms

Combine vinegar, mustard, garlic, shallots, and lemon juice in a blender or food processor; blend thoroughly. Gradually add olive oil and vegetable oil while machine is running. The mixture should emulsify –

come together – into a relatively thick consistency. Season with salt and pepper.

YIELD: 1 cup

P.S. Now is the time to break out the nice olive oil – we cut it with vegetable oil so you don't have to break the bank – but the flavor of the good stuff really stands out!

Buttermilk Dressing

I believe that most Americans – except the mayonnaise haters – have a special (maybe secret) place in their hearts for "ranch" dressing. The creaminess, the tanginess – it really seduces the palate. And that's why we created our own version. We serve it on a wedge of Kurious Farms Bibb lettuce, simply seasoned with salt and pepper. The wedge and the dressing need nothing more than each other! Try it on your favorite salad or as a dip for crudite.

1¼ cups mayonnaise
1 cup buttermilk
2 tablespoons fresh lemon juice
1 tablespoon red wine vinegar
1 teaspoon minced shallot (about ¼ medium shallot)
1 teaspoon freshly ground black pepper
½ teaspoon minced garlic
    (about ½ medium garlic clove)
½ teaspoon hot sauce
½ teaspoon kosher salt

Combine all ingredients in a large bowl; whisk until well blended.

YIELD: About 2½ cups

P.S. This should last for at least a week in your fridge, but the garlic/shallot might start to lose their zest after this point.

Roasted Chicken

Here we offer up our very basic version of this iconic dish! Ours benefits from a nice brine before roasting that ensures juicy, tender meat every time. At the GO we highly recommend brining all fowl and some pork.

One 4- to 5-pound chicken, brined (see recipe below)
1 tablespoon kosher salt
1 tablespoon freshly ground black pepper

Preheat oven to 400 degrees.

Remove the chicken from the brine and pat dry. Rub down chicken with salt and freshly ground black pepper. Place in a roasting pan breast side up and cook on the middle rack of the oven 1 to 1½ hours, until an instant-read thermometer reads 165 degrees when the thigh is probed.

Enjoy as a simple roasted chicken, or allow to cool and pull the meat from the bones, discarding the fat and skin. The meat can be used to make Roasted Chicken Salad (see recipe on page 37) or Chicken and Sausage Jambalaya (see recipe on page 75).

YIELD: 1 roasted chicken

CHICKEN BRINE
One 4- to 5-pound chicken, rinsed
1 cup kosher salt
½ cup sugar
1 teaspoon red pepper flakes
1 teaspoon black peppercorns

1 teaspoon fennel seeds
1 bay leaf
About 20 sprigs of fresh thyme
Few sprigs of fresh rosemary
5 garlic cloves, crushed

Remove chicken from packaging; discard livers, neck, etc. Rinse chicken thoroughly under cold, running water. Combine remaining ingredients with 1 gallon of water in a large pot; simmer until salt and sugar dissolve. Remove from the heat; allow to cool; then add the chicken. Cover and refrigerate for at least 4 and up to 24 hours.

Wes Melling

Wes Melling – Hydroponic Hero

If you are an avid GO diner, you might have noticed a most intriguing cherry tomato garnishing our Straight from the Garden Salad from time to time. It's almost purple – possessing a rather swarthy complexion – and its flavor is even more complex. First comes sweetness followed by a heady, earthy flavor – bringing to mind dark, rich soil. This is most ironic, considering these tomatoes are grown without any dirt whatsoever. Wes and Juanita Melling cultivate these Black Cherry Tomatoes (an heirloom variety) in their entirely hydroponic greenhouse in Moncks Corner.

There at Kurios Farms, they have over 6,000 plants – predominately, lettuce but also tomatoes, cucumbers, and basil. If you have never seen a hydroponic setup, it really is something to behold. From the outside, it might just be another greenhouse – a large white structure made of galvanized metal tubing with a plastic skin. And even when you first enter, it does not look so foreign. Rows upon rows of plants climb up wire trellises, and happy fruit hangs from vines. Bees even flit about, pollinating plants. But then you look down and notice there happens to be no dirt anywhere. Wes grows his plants in perlite – a crushed volcanic rock – and a maze of plastic tubes connects the plants. Water runs through these tubes delivering nutrients like calcium and pot ash, and this entire process is controlled by a silent sentinel that hangs on the front wall.

If you made a quick tour of the place, you might not even notice this Grower's Choice computer, which controls all of the variables – humidity, temperature, feeding, cooling, and air flow. During the height of the season, the plants are fed every 20 minutes for 3 minutes, and they use 1,500 gallons of water each day. It would be easy to give the computer too much credit – a bit like the Wizard in Oz – when, in reality, the Mellings deserve all the credit. They are constantly perusing the rows – harvesting, pruning, and making sure those bees (which they buy bimonthly) are doing their job.

Also, Wes is constantly reprogramming the computer, and he knows better than to blindly trust electronics. One year he noticed that his plants were not progressing at a normal rate, and he finally thought to check his ph meter. He discovered the calibration was off, which meant he was not treating his water correctly, and consequently, he had to rip everything out and start over.

"Every year things come up," says Wes. "You think you have it all under control…"

Still, he would much rather tend to his plants than sit behind a desk. The Mellings moved to South Carolina from Ohio in 1999. Wes had worked in management at BF Goodrich for 12 years when they decided to move away from the cold weather. Originally, the Mellings planned on buying a floral shop in the Charleston area, but that deal fell apart and Wes began to look into other options. He says the hydroponic idea came from a magazine that described how you could make as much money off an eighth of an indoor acre as you could off 100 outdoor acres. Basically, the greenhouse would cost the same as a large tractor.

Wes had always loved gardening, and after visiting a hydroponic setup in Ohio, he decided to take the plunge. For $160,000, www.cropking.com provided all the pieces to build his operation and some technical support. Now, Wes talks casually about seriously scientific-sounding topics like EC, or electrical continuity (which describes the amount of solids in the water) – and he grows exquisite produce.

The Mellings sell their crops from the small storefront connected to the greenhouse and at the Summerville Farmers market. Their season is a bit different from outdoor farming, as it begins in November and ends in July. The plants must be torn out once a year, and July happens to be the perfect time due to the extreme heat and abundance of local tomatoes (which drives the prices down). This alternative growing season works out especially well for restaurants – allowing places like the GO to count on a consistent product during the winter months.

In July, the Mellings might try to take a little break and visit family in Ohio, but like traditional farmers, they are pretty bound to their trade. (They built a home that neighbors the greenhouse.)

"If I didn't enjoy it, I wouldn't do it," Wes says. "If I figured out the time, I would make about $5 per hour."

The Mellings' son, Jarrod, does work with them, and Wes hopes he will take over the bulk of the work in the next few years. For now, his help proves invaluable with the more physical aspects of the job, like walking around on stilts to lower the plants when they reach the top of the trellis. It's idiosyncrasies like this that make hydroponic gardening so unique and add a certain intrigue to the entire process. But when you ask Wes how he most enjoys his own product he gives a simple answer, "The tomatoes are nice sliced, and the lettuce is good on sandwiches," he says.

Dave Merritt and Jaime Tenny

Coast Brewery – Truly Charleston Beer

On a visit to Coast Brewery in North Charleston, South Carolina, you will find husband-and-wife team Dave Merritt and Jaime Tenny busy at work. They might be brewing, bottling, meeting with their distributor, or doing endless amounts of cleaning. They take their business of crafting premium beer seriously. That said, they also do business on their terms. The Grateful Dead might be playing softly in the background, and they might stop to throw the ball to their friendly mutt, "Teach" (named for the pirate Edward Teach, aka Blackbeard).

Dave and Jaime have been operating their own brewery since September 2007, and Lowcountry beer enthusiasts recognize them as the local leaders in their field. Of course, like so many good stories, theirs came about seemingly by happenstance. Dave might say it all started in 1994, during their senior year at Wando High School, when Jaime moved to Charleston from New Jersey.

"And I didn't like him!" says Jaime, finishing Dave's story for him.

She might say it started when they began dating during her sophomore year at College of Charleston. Regardless, by 1997, they had their first son, Kai, and Dave had made his fateful trip to a home brewing shop.

Jaime says he began home brewing simply because he wanted better tasting beer, but that casual interest quickly evolved. In 1998, Dave headed out to the American Brewers Guild in Davis, California. He completed the five months of coursework, but he had to forego the internship.

"By this point, we only had like $5," says Jaime with a good-natured laugh.

So Dave returned to his family in Charleston and began working at Southend Brewery. There he worked with head brewer, Frank Hughes, who soon became his mentor. During his 18 months at Southend, Dave learned and experimented – crafting beers far ahead of that time. But when the leading local brewery – Palmetto – sought Dave out to be their head brewer in 1999, he could not say no.

At Palmetto there was no experimentation, but the job brought a degree of stability to the young family. And in 2001, Jaime had their second son, Aiden. Dave remained at Palmetto for over nine years and even kept his position during the first two years of opening Coast.

As Dave honed his craft, Jaime was "busy raising kids, " but she did find the time to develop her own palate. She clearly remembers her beer epiphany: drinking an Avery Maharaja around 2000. She calls it her "gateway beer" and can still recount her flood of emotions.

"Holy cow! Oh my god! What are hops? I really like them."

Her genuine love for good beer inspired her to challenge South Carolina's law that prohibited the brewing or selling of a beer with an alcohol content over six percent. In 2005, Jaime founded Pop the Cap – a group made up of South Carolina brewers – who began lobbying the state government to change the law. When they achieved their goal in 2007, it really paved the road to the opening of Coast.

Jaime and Dave both laugh now thinking back to the antiquated law. Only three out of the twenty-nine beers they have brewed thus far would have been legal according to that law. Another victory came in June 2010, when the government deemed it legal for breweries to conduct tastings and sell a limited amount of beer on their premises. So on Thursdays, from 4 to 7 p.m., and on Saturdays, from 11 a.m. to 2 p.m., Jaime and Dave sample folks on their latest creations and their staples, like HopArt IPA and 32/50 Kolsch.

After overcoming so many hurdles, it's understandable that Jaime and Dave seem so carefree these days. Their happiness radiates off of them with the ease that comes when you find your way. Sure, the brew days still stretch out over 14 hours, and they only have a bit of part time help. But they are operating by their rules. They use organic ingredients, run the brewery on biodiesel, and send their spent grain to a local farm. They sell 99 percent of their beer in Charleston and don't see that changing anytime soon.

Investors have approached them about expanding their operations, but they like the size of their business. Dave brews every batch, and they bottle the beer together. They banter back and forth all day.

"It's definitely what he's meant to do," says Jaime.

"It's not that difficult," says Dave.

"When your gifted," she replies.

* * *

At the GO, we are proud to serve HopArt as our only draft beer, and with every pitcher you receive a complimentary basket of fries and bearnaise.

CHAPTER 2

Soups, Salads and Other Stuff

Jennie Ruth's Deviled Eggs

These deviled eggs are a tribute to my partner Chris Stewart's grandmother, Jennie Ruth. She was an inspiration to his cooking with her classic Southern ways, and here you see that tradition shining through. We do add some GO flair to this recipe with Chris's Thunder Sauce (a sweet pepper relish), but plain old sweet pickle relish works just fine. In fact, that's what Jennie Ruth used!

Read Jennie Ruth's story on page 39.

6 large eggs
2½ tablespoons Thunder Sauce, or sweet pickle relish
1 tablespoon mayonnaise
1 tablespoon yellow mustard
1½ teaspoons hot sauce

Bring a medium pot of water to a boil. Add eggs; boil for 14 minutes. Have a bowl of ice water ready. Transfer eggs to this ice bath. Once cool, remove from water and peel. Slice eggs in half lengthwise and carefully remove the yolks. Add the yolks, Thunder Sauce (or pickle relish), mayonnaise, yellow mustard, and hot sauce to the bowl of a blender or food processor; run until smooth. Alternatively, combine these ingredients in a medium bowl and work together using a fork until relatively smooth. Spoon into the whites.

YIELD: 12 Deviled Eggs

P.S. You can make your own sweet pickle relish by pureeing some of our Housemade Pickles (see page 96) in a blender or food processor.

P.P.S. We also believe our deviled eggs stand out because of the eggs themselves. They come from the happy hens of Celeste and George Albers. Read their story on page 165.

Pimento Cheese

I am crazy about pimento cheese, and so I naturally put some heart into creating our version. Obviously, this is a simple treat, but sometimes simple is best. My only stipulation is that Duke's mayonnaise makes a delicious difference!

At the GO, we serve this on brioche from Normandy Farms Bakery as a grilled sandwich, and at brunch, as an omelette, but all you really need are some nice buttery crackers for a perfect snack.

2 cups grated sharp cheddar
½ cup canned or jarred pimento peppers, drained
    and chopped
¼ cup chopped green onions
½ cup mayonnaise
1 teaspoon freshly ground black pepper
½ teaspoon kosher salt
¼ teaspoon cayenne
Dash of hot sauce

Combine cheddar, pimentos, and green onions in a medium bowl; set aside. Combine mayonnaise, pepper, salt, cayenne, and hot sauce in a medium bowl; whisk together. Add mayonnaise to cheese mixture; gently stirring together using a rubber spatula until thoroughly combined. (The only real mistake you can make here is overworking the pimento cheese; hence, we suggest that you "gently stir.")

YIELD: Serves 4 to 6 as an appetizer; about 3 cups

Amazing Chili

Sometimes you need a timeless classic, and that's this dish. There are so many varieties of chili, each with their own merits, but my partner Chris swears by his straightforward rendition. At the GO, we serve it over locally made cavatelli pasta as our own "souped up" Chili Mac!

2 pounds ground pork
½ cup finely chopped bacon (about 5 ounces or 4 to 5 standard grocery store slices)
2 cups chopped onion (about 1 medium onion)
1 cup chopped celery (about 3 medium stalks)
1 cup chopped green bell pepper (about 1 bell pepper)
¹/₃ cup sliced garlic (about 6 medium garlic cloves)
1 tablespoon kosher salt
2 tablespoons chili powder
2 tablespoons cumin
1½ tablespoons paprika
1 teaspoon oregano
½ teaspoon freshly ground white pepper
½ teaspoon freshly ground black pepper
½ teaspoon toasted fennel seed, ground in spice grinder
Pinch of cayenne
Pinch of cinnamon
Pinch of ground nutmeg
Pinch of ground clove
Two 28-ounce cans crushed tomatoes
Two 27-ounce cans red kidney beans, drained and rinsed

About 20 sprigs of fresh thyme, tied in a bundle with kitchen twine
1 bay leaf
Grated sharp cheddar cheese, for garnish
Sour cream, for garnish
Green onions, for garnish
Hot sauce, for garnish

Heat a large pot over high heat. Add ground pork and bacon; cook, breaking up with a wooden spoon, until well browned, about 20 minutes. (Meat will release water. Once water evaporates, the meat will begin to brown. Keep running the spoon over the bottom of the pot to release any bits collecting there. This nice, caramelized meat is referred to as "fond.") Reduce heat to medium-high. Add onion, celery, bell pepper, garlic, salt, and spices. The vegetables will also release water that will allow you to scrape even more fond from the bottom of the pot. Cook until onions are translucent, about 10 minutes. Add crushed tomatoes, kidney beans, thyme, bay leaf, and one quart of water; simmer for an hour. Serve with cheddar cheese, sour cream, green onions, and hot sauce, to taste.

YIELD: About 12 servings; about 4 quarts

P.S. Chris loves his chili with lots of beans, but feel free to cut back if you prefer less.

Chilled Corn Soup

We serve this soup at the height of summer, using beautiful white corn. The simple list of ingredients ensures that the essence of the corn shines through.

7 ears white corn, shucked
2 tablespoons vegetable oil
2 cups chopped onion (about 1 medium onion)
2 cups peeled and chopped russet potato (about 1 medium russet potato)
2 cups heavy cream
1 tablespoon plus 1 teaspoon kosher salt
2 teaspoons freshly ground white pepper
½ teaspoon cayenne
Honey, to taste (optional)

Cut corn off the cob; set aside. In a large pot, cover ears with water. Simmer for 1 hour. Remove from the heat and strain through a colander into a large bowl. (Should reduce to about 7 cups of "corn water.")

Heat oil in a large pot over medium heat. Add onions; cook until translucent, about 10 minutes. Add corn and corn water; bring to a boil. Add potatoes and cream; simmer until potato is tender, about 15 minutes. Allow to cool.

Working in batches, puree corn mixture in a blender. Have a chinois placed in a bowl nearby. Once the soup is pureed, ladle it from the blender into the chinois. Some will go through quite easily. For the rest, you will need to force it through using the ladle. Holding the chinois in one hand, over the bowl, and the ladle in the other, gently push through the mixture to the bottom of the chinois repeatedly. You will eventually be left with nothing but corn pulp, which you can discard. Repeat this process until you have pureed all of the corn mixture.

Season with salt, white pepper, and cayenne. If it is not the peak of corn season, you can add some honey to make up for the missing sweetness – starting with 1 teaspoon, but up to 1 tablespoon should do the trick.

Cover and refrigerate until cold, about 2 hours.

YIELD: 8 to 10 servings; about 2 quarts

P.S. You can easily halve this recipe!

P.P.S. Don't let the term "chinois" scare vou awav from the recipe. This is simply a conical, fine-meshed strainer that should be available at your local cookware store or definitely online. It is not that expensive and is essential any time you are looking for a pristine, velvety texture, such as here with a pureed soup or in the "Sweets Chapter" for puddings. Other fine-meshed strainers can also work, but when dealing with larger quantities, the chinois is ideal.

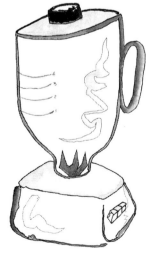

Chicken Liver Mousse

After much deliberation, we decided to share our recipe for sublimely elegant Chicken Liver Mousse. Here you will find a starter that will blow your guests away, but be forewarned: you need a few special tools. First, you will need a pate terrine. This might seem like a frivolous investment, but it enables you to delve into a whole new realm of cooking. Second, you will do yourself a favor by going out to your local whole-sale warehouse (think Sam's or Costco) and buying some commercial plastic wrap. While the grocery store variety will work, you will find the heavier-duty stuff proves much easier to manage for lining your terrine and for wrapping up all your leftovers! Finally, you will need to order "pink" curing salt from a web-site, unless you happen to have a genuine butcher that can provide you with some. This preservative is a necessity, as it will keep your mousse a beautiful, rosy shade in the center as opposed to dull, brown-ish gray. One website to check out is www.butcher-packer.com for this and other cool charcuterie items.

Now, the rest should be a breeze. Just be sure to check your mousse after about 40 minutes to make sure all is going well. Serve with our Housemade Pickles (see recipe on page 100), Creole mustard (or other whole grain mustard), and butter crackers.

1 pound chicken livers
2 cups buttermilk
Vegetable oil, for greasing terrine
4 large eggs
2 tablespoons kosher salt

2 tablespoons freshly ground white pepper
½ teaspoon "pink" salt (see head note)
1 quart heavy cream

Combine livers and buttermilk in a medium bowl.
Cover and refrigerate overnight.

Preheat oven to 325 degrees.

Grease a 1½-quart pate terrine with vegetable oil;
line with plastic wrap.

Remove livers from buttermilk and rinse in a colander under running water. Transfer them to a blender
or food processor and puree until smooth. Add eggs,
salt, white pepper, and "pink" salt; pulse to combine.
Add 2 cups of heavy cream; pulse to combine. Strain
mixture through a chinos or other fine-meshed strainer
into a large bowl. A ladle will help you push the mixture
through the strainer. Add remaining 2 cups cream;
whisk to combine. Pour mixture into the terrine. Place
the terrine in a roasting pan and put into oven. Fill a
large bowl with scalding hot water and pour into roasting pan until the water comes three-quarters of the
way up the side of the terrine. (This is a water bath!)

Bake mousse until mixture is firm
when jiggled, 50 minutes to
1 hour. Allow to cool. Refrigerate
until completely cold. Remove
from refrigerator, run a paring
knife around the edges of the
mousse, and invert to release on
a baking sheet or serving tray.

If the mousse will not release, allow to warm slightly (about 15 minutes) and then it should release easily.

YIELD: About 12 generous slabs; enough to be served as an hors d'oeuvre at a 40-person cocktail party.

Peel-n-Eat Boiled Shrimp

There is nothing easier or more tasty than fresh shrimp boiled with some seasonings, and we've figured out the perfect medley so that you can impress all your friends!

12 cups water
$^2/_3$ cup white wine
$^2/_3$ cup kosher salt
2 tablespoons mustard seed
1 tablespoon cayenne
1 teaspoon red pepper flakes
1 teaspoon coriander seed
1 teaspoon black peppercorns
About 20 sprigs of fresh thyme
½ cup roughly chopped celery (about 1½ medium
    stalks)
1 onion, quartered
1 lemon, halved, juices and actual fruit used
4 garlic cloves, crushed
3 pounds shrimp, unpeeled

Combine all ingredients excluding shrimp in a large pot and bring to a boil. Add shrimp and cook until just done, about 3 to 5 minutes. Shrimp should be pink and firm. Drain – do not rinse! Serve as "peel-n-eat" with our cocktail sauce (see recipe on page 5) or red remoulade (see recipe on page 6).

YIELD: 8 appetizer portions

Roasted Chicken Salad

At the GO, you will find no grapes, nuts, or herbs in our chicken salad – just delicious roasted chicken dressed the old-fashioned way. Imagine sitting at the drugstore lunch counter or in your grandmother's kitchen and savoring this classic rendition on toasted white bread – that's our chicken salad!

We serve this as an opened-faced po boy with some of our Housemade Pickles (see recipe on page 96) and one of Jennie Ruth's Deviled Eggs (see recipe on page 24).

½ cup celery (about 1½ medium stalks)
½ cup mayonnaise
¼ cup Creole mustard
1½ teaspoons hot sauce
1½ teaspoons red wine vinegar
½ teaspoon kosher salt
½ teaspoon freshly ground black pepper
Pulled meat from a 4- to 5- pound roasted
    chicken, about 4½ cups (see recipe on page 10)

Combine celery, mayonnaise, mustard, hot sauce, vinegar, salt, and pepper in a large bowl; stir to combine. Add chicken; mix until thoroughly incorporated. Serve on bed of lettuce or as a sandwich.

YIELD: 4 to 5 cups; about 4 servings

Jennie Ruth Stewart

Jennie Ruth – A Tribute
1914-1991

This piece was written by my partner Chris Stewart's father, Tom, telling us about the person for whom we named our deviled eggs: his mother, Jennie Ruth.

* * *

Jennie Ruth Haley was born on August 1, 1914 in Crystal Springs, Mississippi. Crystal Springs is about half way between Jackson, Mississippi and New Orleans – basically in the heart of the Mississippi Delta. She was born on a farm, the seventh child of Oliver and Belle Haley. Her father died when she was three years old, and subsequently, her oldest brother, Wade, moved to Birmingham, Alabama to find work. Shortly thereafter, he moved the rest of the family to Birmingham.

All of the brothers and sisters worked at whatever jobs they could find and pooled the money so the family could stay together. During the depression, they opened a small restaurant and served "southern food" – what natives call "meat-and-three" type food. Jennie Ruth had three brothers and three sisters. All of the sisters learned to cook from their mother, Belle, who ran the kitchen in the restaurant. The brothers worked as servers, dishwashers, etc. All of the sisters became excellent cooks, and their love of food lasted throughout their lives.

Jennie Ruth married Calvin Stewart in 1937, and after the war, they had two children: my brother Jim and me. Calvin was born in LaFayette, Alabama on a farm. His family moved to Birmingham in the 1920s. Calvin believed that one of the immutable laws of nature is that if you own any piece of land you must grow something on it. No back yard was complete without a garden. From the time they were married until Calvin died in 1985, he never owned a home without a vegetable garden in the back yard. After he retired, he convinced a friend to let him "farm" a vacant lot owned by the friend and close to his home, so that he had two gardens.

In these gardens, he grew every vegetable he could grow in Birmingham. Corn, butterbeans, green beans, okra, cucumbers, tomatoes, and turnip greens were the staples. Bell peppers, banana peppers, and occasionally watermelons also appeared. He loved to work in the dirt; he loved to see things grow; he loved to give the excess away; and most of all he loved to eat the results of his hard work.

And Jennie Ruth loved to cook the fruits and vegetables which came out of Calvin's garden. Her meals were legendary in the family. A typical Sunday dinner would consist of fried chicken, roast beef, and a ham. On a very special day, country fried steak would join the menu. Rice and gravy, creamed corn, green beans, squash, field peas, butter beans, sliced tomatoes, onions, bell peppers, those famous "Jennie Ruth's Deviled Eggs," and always corn bread would complete the menu. Dessert would be either peach, blackberry, or apple cobbler. There would be pound cake in the home 90 percent of the time, year in and year out. And there were usually homemade cookies of one type or another.

Summer trips to the local farmers market would result in bushels of green beans, corn, and butter beans. These would be shelled immediately, no matter how late you had to stay up to finish, and then canned for the winter. Thanksgiving and Christmas were simply orgies of food. All of the sisters would cook their best dishes and the family would eat themselves comatose.

My brother and I took this cornucopia of food for granted. We never knew until we were adults, that for some people, macaroni and cheese comes from a box and green beans come from a can. We grew to appreciate our mother's ways in the kitchen when we began to see that what other people called "good food" was, in reality, food that Jennie Ruth would never serve to a stranger.

All of the Stewarts have fond memories of Jennie Ruth for lots of reasons. But the central memory is of the wonderful food which she lovingly prepared and served to her family. She enjoyed nothing more in life than seeing her family enjoy themselves eating the fresh, locally grown food that she prepared from scratch.

Fred Dockery

Fred Dockery – Lowcountry Waterman

Fred Dockery defies an easy definition. He comes to the shrimping and crabbing business not by birth but by choice. He comes armed with a degree in philosophy and an impeccable fluency in the French language. But the waters cast their spell on him years ago. Now, he utterly depends on them just like the multi-generational fishing families he works alongside. It's not simply a job but a way of life.

However, Fred does bring a unique attitude to this passion, and it's an attitude cultivated by his rich and varied upbringing – beginning in Montpellier, France. There, in 1964, his single mother, a Portuguese psychologist gave birth to Fred. Shortly thereafter, she met a young American man who happened to be in the area on a Fulbright scholarship. They fell in love, married, and moved to America in 1968. His adopted father's career as a French professor kept the family on the move – from North Carolina to Iowa to Maine and finally back to North Carolina. Fred even spent another year in France where he spoke the language as if he had never left, and even now his eyes light up when he talks of France.

Eventually, Fred found himself at Bates College in Maine where he studied philosophy simply out of interest. Like so many youth on the cusp of adulthood, he had no idea what he really wanted to do. After college he tried his hand at screenwriting in New York City and environmental education in Connecticut. When neither panned out to his liking, he found himself living in an old airplane hangar on the Connecticut coast contemplating his next move. He also found himself hungry, and when one of his "housemates" offered up his position on a commercial fishing boat Fred started work the next day. He still remembers that first seasick morning out on the water; he loved it.

As it turns out, Fred entered the New England fishing scene at a dynamic time – the end of the "lobster-trawler wars." Territorial rights play a significant role in commercial fishing, and here the lobstermen believed that the big trawlers had infringed on theirs. Within his first month, the lobstermen fired shots and sunk the 40-foot trawler that employeed Fred. The crew pulled the boat up and repaired it, but the captain had fought his last battle. He offered the job up, and with one month's experience Fred began running his own boat.

"It was like setting a kid loose in a gravel pit with a backhoe!" he says, smiling broadly.

Fred worked various fishing jobs until he met his wife, Catherine, in 1987. They decided to move back down South, closer to both their families, and wound up in Charleston. Fred found work at Atlantic Clam Farms and remained there from 1991 to 1996. After clamming, he tried his hand at oystering, but the work wreaked havoc on his back. Next, Fred turned to crabbing and eventually shrimping. He laughs now, remembering his first attempt at shrimping.

"I had no idea what I was doing," he says. "I was measuring [my catch] in numbers not pounds."

Thankfully, veteran shrimper Neal Cooksey took Fred under his tutelage – selling him an old net and introducing him to tricks of the trade like the "tickle chain." On his next trip out, he found success – catching so many shrimp that he ran out of coolers and ice.

These days, his catch can vary from less than a pound to 40 pounds, but Fred does not have quite the stress of the big trawlers. He goes out on a 19-foot skiff, which burns only a fraction of the fuel, and he can crab on the same day. Of course, it's not easy work. Fred goes out most days by himself – hauling in heavy nets and crab traps. And he hauls them in knowing the sad reality of a market flooded by cheap, imported shrimp. Fred believes that the only real answer to this issue would be taxing these shrimp from Asia and South America or creating government subsidies for American fishermen. Simply put, he likes the grassroots campaigns, but he believes they are just not enough.

"It is not a wasted lesson teaching the value of fresh and local, but people shop with their pocketbooks, and the bulk of them still want big shrimp at a low price," he says.

In addition to such larger issues, Fred also still deals with the territorial drama that seems unavoidable in the fishing business. Feuds between crabbers result in lines to identifying buoys being cut – meaning a loss of crabs, equipment, and time. Fred tries to stay out of such disputes because one can never be sure who victimized you.

"If I retaliated, remorse would eat me up," he says.

Besides, Fred does not come across as a fighter. In fact, he seems genuinely happy despite the long hours and low pay. He recognizes that this is a life he chose for himself and his family. He and Catherine have three children – Carlisle, Evan, and Emma – all old enough to de-head and sort shrimp. Only one – his son Evan – has a real interest in the business. He goes

out with Fred on most weekends and even saved up
to buy his own boat at age 10.

When asked whether he wonders if Evan would
be better off choosing another path, Fred laughs.

"I don't have to wonder; I know he would be better off," he says. "I would be better off too! But on a
day like today, where else would I rather be?"

He waves his arm motioning to the world around
him – the sweetgrass whispers; a few white, pictur-
esque clouds float lazily in the blue sky; Spanish moss
hangs from the oak trees ; herons and egrets soar
gracefully; red-winged blackbirds and purple martins
flit about; and a gentle, breeze strikes up, as if on cue.

* * *

At the GO we buy shrimp, blue crabs, and stone
crabs from Fred, and they all represent the supreme
quality that only local seafood can offer.

CHAPTER 3

Plates

Mustard Fried Catfish

Let's be upfront – frying seafood at home is just not that easy. This is why we have chosen to include a recipe, only for fried catfish, versus fried shrimp or oysters. The catfish is a little more forgiving, and it is truly unique because of our mustard marinade. Plus, there are few parties more fun than a fish fry. To turn this into a party, simply double the recipe, fire up your gas camp stove, and set up on your porch or deck. Line the table with old newspapers, and you are in business. The reality is that fried seafood is best straight out of the oil, and the party setting allows you to serve folks immediately. Just be sure to snag a couple of pieces for yourself and have an assistant handy with cold beverages!

2 pounds catfish filets, boneless
1 cup yellow mustard
1 cup Creole mustard, or other whole grain mustard
Vegetable oil for frying
2 cups all-purpose flour
1½ cups yellow cornmeal
1½ cups corn starch
1½ tablespoons kosher salt
1 tablespoon freshly ground black pepper
1 tablespoon freshly ground white pepper
1 teaspoon cayenne

Combine catfish, yellow mustard, and Creole mustard in a large bowl and toss with your hands until the catfish is thoroughly coated. Cover and refrigerate for at least 4 and up to 24 hours.

Preheat oven to 200 degrees.

Heat 4 inches of oil to 375 degrees in a large pot. (A skillet can also be used, but the pot helps reduce splattering!)

Combine flour, cornmeal, corn starch, salt, black pepper, white pepper, and cayenne in a large bowl; whisk to combine. Dredge catfish through flour mixture and transfer to a wire rack set over a baking sheet.

Using tongs, carefully drop two filets at a time into oil and fry until breading is very crispy, about 2 minutes per side. Transfer filets to a paper-lined baking sheet, season with additional salt and pepper (to taste), and hold in the oven as you fry the remaining pieces of catfish.

Serve with GO cocktail, tartar, or remoulade sauce! (See recipes in Chapter 1.)

YIELD: 4 to 6 servings

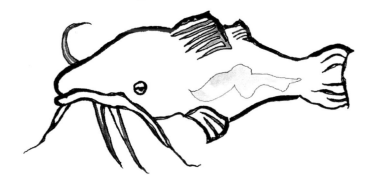

Papa's Oyster Stew

Growing up, every holiday season my father and I would go buy a Christmas tree together, and then we would buy quarts of freshly shucked oysters to make his famous stew while trimming the tree. Freshly shucked oysters may seem a bit incongruous if you remember that my hometown is the extremely inland hamlet of Columbus, Georgia. But my father's good friends, the Lunsfords, owned Rose Hill Seafood, where they brought in oysters straight from Apalachicola, Florida. The flavor of those oysters, and especially this stew, is the flavor of my childhood.

1 quart shucked oysters and their liquor
3 tablespoons unsalted butter
2 cups chopped onion (about 1 medium onion)
1 teaspoon kosher salt, more to taste
2 teaspoons freshly ground black pepper
3 cups milk
1 cup heavy cream
Oyster crackers, for garnish

Place the oysters in a colander set over a bowl to drain off liquor. Reserve liquor and oysters.

Melt butter in a medium pot over medium heat. When foam subsides, add the onions, salt, and pepper. Cook until onions are translucent, about 10 minutes. Add the reserved oyster liquor and cook until reduced by half, about 10 minutes. Add the milk and cream; bring to a simmer. Add the oysters; cook until their outer edges begin to curl, about 5 minutes. Serve hot with oyster crackers.

YIELD: About 4 entree servings

P.S. The stew might require more salt, depending on the salinity of the oysters, but it is best not to oversalt at the outset.

P.P.S. I love a lot of black pepper in creamy dishes like this stew, but feel free to use less than the recommended 2 teaspoons if your palate is sensitive to spice.

Summertime Shrimp and Grits

Here we take the classic New Orleans dish Shrimp Creole and serve it over grits. Upon first opening, we tried serving it over rice – in keeping with Louisiana tradition – but in Charleston folks really love their shrimp and grits! Either way, it's delicious!

5 medium tomatoes
1 tablespoon vegetable oil
2 cups diced onion (about 1 medium onion)
1 cup diced green bell pepper (about 1 large bell pepper)
1 cup diced celery (about 3 medium stalks)
2 tablespoons sliced garlic (about 2 medium garlic cloves)
1 tablespoon kosher salt
1 teaspoon dried oregano
½ teaspoon freshly ground black pepper
½ teaspoon freshly ground white pepper
¼ teaspoon red pepper flakes
Pinch of cayenne
½ cup tomato paste
About 20 sprigs of fresh thyme, tied in a bundle with kitchen twine
1 bay leaf
1 pound shrimp, peeled and deveined

Bring a large pot of water to a boil. Have a bowl of ice water nearby. Remove core from tomatoes with a paring knife. Score opposite end with an "x" and drop into boiling water. Cook until skin just begins to pull back, 1 to 2 minutes. Remove from pot and submerge in bowl of ice water. Once cool, peel off skin and slice tomatoes into quarters.

Heat oil in a large pot over medium heat. Add onion, peppers, celery, and garlic. Cook, stirring, until onions are translucent, about 10 minutes. Add salt, oregano, black pepper, white pepper, red pepper flakes, and cayenne; stir to thoroughly combine. Add tomatoes, tomato paste, thyme, and the bay leaf; stir to thoroughly combine. Cover pan and reduce to low heat. Simmer, stirring occasionally, until sauce comes together, about 1 hour.

Add shrimp and cook until just pink and firm, about 5 minutes. Discard thyme and bay leaf before serving. Serve over grits (see recipe on page 102).

YIELD: 4 to 6 servings

Shrimp Cakes

Our shrimp cakes came to be when we ended up with a bounty of delicious creek shrimp from Alabama. These tiny shrimp come from tidal creeks in the marshlands and, because of their size, are perfect for forming into cakes. Here I call for medium shrimp, as they are easier to come by. Just be sure to take extra care in finely chopping the shrimp and all of your vegetables.

At the GO, we like to serve these over grits with a field pea salad or at brunch topped with poached eggs!

¼ cup vegetable oil
¼ cup finely diced onion (about ¼ small onion)
¼ cup finely diced green bell pepper (about ¼ medium bell pepper)
¼ cup finely diced red bell pepper (about ¼ medium bell pepper)
1 pound boiled shrimp (see recipe below)
1 large egg
3 tablespoons heavy cream
½ teaspoon kosher salt
1 tablespoon hot sauce
2 tablespoons Creole mustard, or other whole grain mustard
½ cup plain bread crumbs
1 cup panko (Japanese bread crumbs), optional

Preheat oven to 500 degrees.

Heat 1 tablespoon vegetable oil in a skillet over medium heat. Add onions and bell peppers and cook until onions are translucent, about 5 minutes. Remove from heat and allow to cool.

Chop shrimp finely. (At the restaurant, we use a food processor, but it is possible to accomplish this recipe with simply a knife or by pulsing the shrimp in a blender.)

Combine shrimp, cooked vegetables, egg, cream, salt, hot sauce, and mustard in a large bowl; work together with your hands. Add bread crumbs in $1/8$ cup increments until mixture is just dry enough to form into cakes. (Less is more in this case. If you use too many bread crumbs, your cakes will be dry and fall apart.)

To coat your cakes in panko, simply have panko in a shallow baking dish and then dredge your cakes through it.

Heat 2 tablespoons vegetable oil in a skillet over medium-high heat. Add cakes, two at a time, and cook until well browned on both sides, about 2 minutes per side. (Add remaining tablespoon of oil to pan if necessary during the cooking process.) Transfer cakes to a baking sheet or dish and bake for 5 minutes.

Serve with Tartar Sauce or Red Remoulade (see recipes on page 4 and page 6).

Yield: 8 4-ounce cakes

P.S. A note on breadcrumbs. In this recipe we call for two types of breadcrumbs. First, we call for ordinary breadcrumbs to mix with the cakes. You may use the store-bought variety, but we highly recommend making your own by processing stale bread in a blender or food processor. Second, we call for panko to coat the cakes before cooking them. These Japanese bread crumbs are a great restaurant trick for creating an extra crisp crust on certain fried foods. While the shrimp cakes will taste just fine without them, you can wow your guests if you have some on hand!

SIMPLIFIED BOILED SHRIMP
6 cups water
$1/3$ cup white wine
$1/3$ cup kosher salt
1 tablespoon mustard seed
1½ teaspoons cayenne
½ teaspoon red pepper flakes
½ teaspoon black peppercorns
About 20 sprigs of fresh thyme, tied in a bundle with kitchen twine
½ onion, quartered
½ lemon, juices and actual fruit used
2 garlic cloves, crushed
1 pound medium shrimp, peeled and deveined

Combine all ingredients in a large pot and bring to a boil. Add shrimp and cook until just pink and firm, about 3 minutes. Drain – do not rinse! Allow to cool and reserve for use in shrimp cakes.

P.S. As the name states, this is a more simplified court bouillon (that's a fancy word for poaching liquid) than the one you will find in Chapter 1. Since these shrimp will be combined with even more ingredients and seasoning after cooking, we cut you a little slack on the grocery list for this court bouillon!

Crawfish Etouffee

Most would refer to this as a classic Cajun dish – meaning that its roots lie in the countryside southwest of New Orleans. *Etouffer* means "to smother" in French, which seems like a good connotation for this light stew. We keep ours pretty traditional – starting with a roux, going in with your trinity (onions, celery, bell pepper), and finishing with the crawfish. You wind up with a heartwarming meal in very little time.

5 tablespoons unsalted butter
½ cup all-purpose flour
1 cup chopped onion (about ½ medium onion)
½ cup chopped celery (about 1½ medium stalks)
½ cup chopped green bell pepper (about ½ large
    bell pepper)
1 teaspoon kosher salt
1 teaspoon dried oregano
½ teaspoon freshly ground black pepper
½ teaspoon freshly ground white pepper
Pinch of cayenne
Pinch of red pepper flakes
1 tablespoon minced garlic (about 3 medium garlic
    cloves)
1 quart chicken stock or canned low-sodium chicken
    broth
About 20 sprigs of fresh thyme, tied together with
    kitchen twine
1 pound crawfish tails, cooked
½ cup chopped green onions
1 teaspoon hot sauce
Steamed white rice, for serving

Heat a large pot over medium heat. Add 4 tablespoons of butter and melt. Add ¼ cup flour and cook, stirring constantly, until your roux has become a caramel color, about 10 minutes. Add remaining ¼ cup flour; stir to combine. Add onion, celery, and bell pepper; stir to combine. Add salt, oregano, black pepper, white pepper, cayenne, and red pepper flakes. Cook until onions are translucent, about 10 minutes. Add garlic and cook until fragrant, about 30 seconds. Add stock and thyme and bring to a simmer. Cook until reduced by half, about 30 minutes. Add crawfish, green onions, remaining tablespoon of butter, and hot sauce; stir to combine. Cook until crawfish are hot to touch, about 3 minutes.

Discard thyme bundle before serving.

Serve over steamed white rice with hot sauce for garnish.

Yield: 4 servings

P.S. You can easily order frozen crawfish tails online if they are not available in your area. We order ours from www.lacrawfish.com – and they are superb. You can also substitute a pound of shrimp – adding them with your green onions, butter, and hot sauce and cooking them until they are just pink and firm, about 5 minutes.

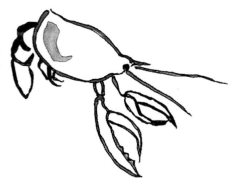

Anne's Grillades and Grits

If one dish could epitomize New Orleans comfort food, I would place my bet on grillades (pronounced "gree-yadz"). Many associate it with brunch, but my partner Charles most enjoyed it for his birthday dinner. His mother, Anne, made hers with beef, but lots of New Orleanians would insist on veal. Defying both these traditions, we make ours with pork butt, which happens to be very affordable and flavorful. Serve this dish in the depths of a cold, dreary winter when you have nothing better to do than cook the day away. You will be sure to win many fans!

2 cups red wine
3½ pounds pork butt, diced
2 tablespoons plus 1 teaspoon kosher salt
1 tablespoon plus 1 teaspoon freshly ground black pepper
¼ cup vegetable oil
¼ to ½ cup all-purpose flour
3 cups chopped onion (about 1½ medium onions or 1 large onion)
2 cups chopped green bell pepper (about 2½ medium bell peppers)
2 cups chopped celery (about 3 medium stalks)
1 quart chicken stock or canned low-sodium chicken broth
1 28-ounce can crushed tomatoes
¼ cup hot sauce
1½ tablespoons Worcestershire Sauce
About 20 sprigs of fresh thyme, tied in a bundle with kitchen twine
1 tablespoon dried oregano

2 bay leaves
4 garlic cloves, crushed

Bring wine to a boil in a medium saucepan and reduce by half. Reserve for later use.

Season pork with 1 tablespoon salt and 1 tablespoon pepper. Heat a large cast iron Dutch oven or other large pot over medium-high heat. Add pork butt and sear until all of the meat is well browned and has released some fat, 10 to 20 minutes. (Be sure to turn meat over once browned so that all sides brown evenly. You are looking for a dark caramel color.) Transfer the meat to a large baking dish and reserve for later use.

Reduce heat to medium. (Be sure to allow the pot's temperature to lower a bit so that you do not immediately burn the flour. This will also calm down the spitting and spatting that the leftover pork bits are most likely doing.) Add oil and enough flour to form a thin paste. (Amount of flour will depend on amount of fat released from pork butt. If it released a lot of fat, you could need up to ½ cup flour. This is your "roux"!) Cook, stirring constantly, until your roux has become dark chocolate brown in color, 15 to 20 minutes. This obviously takes a little while and is a very important part of the process. The key with a roux is patience. If you try to speed up the process by increasing the heat, you risk burning the roux. This will ruin the entire dish, as it is the foundation of the flavor. Simply relax and stir. Also, be careful of splashing yourself with the roux, as it is molten hot!

Once you have achieved desired color, add the onions, bell peppers, and celery to the pot. Season with remaining 4 teaspoons of salt and 1 teaspoon of black pepper. Saute until onions are translucent, about 10 minutes. Add the reserved wine, stock, tomatoes, hot sauce, Worcestershire, thyme, oregano, bay leaves, garlic, and reserved pork; stir to combine. Bring to a boil, reduce to a simmer, and cook until meat is very tender (it should begin to shred when prodded with a fork), about 3 hours. Discard thyme bundle and bay leaves before serving.

Serve over grits (see recipe on page 102).

YIELD: About 8 servings

P.S. This is a recipe where it is important to understand the meaning of "simmer." In order for the meat to actually break down, the stew should be moderately bubbling rather than simply steaming over a very low flame. Vigorous bubbling connotes boiling; moderate bubbling connotes simmering.

P.P.S. At the GO, we often add shrimp to this dish to create our Wintertime Shrimp and Grits. To do this, simply add one pound of peeled and deveined shrimp as the last step in the cooking process (once your meat is fork tender). Stir and cook until shrimp are just pink and firm, about 5 minutes. This will increase your yield – giving you 10 to 12 servings. You will want to double the grits recipe in this circumstance!

Stew's Meatloaf

At the GO, we often have meatloaf on the menu because my partner Chris (AKA "Stew") happens to make the best meatloaf around. We generally serve it as a po boy, but here we give you a very tasty tomato sauce so that you can serve it over mashed potatoes – or for something different, try serving it over grits!

At first glance, this recipe might seem, a no-brainer, but there is finesse involved. The key is to not over-work the meatloaf mixture. At the restaurant, we accomplish this by putting everything – meat, vegetables, spices, etc. – through the meat grinder. If you happen to have a home grinder, feel free to use this method. Another alternative would be to ask your butcher to grind the beef and pork together, but you can always just use your hands. Simply remember: work together gently, using a folding rather than a kneading motion!

And just like our shrimp cakes, we call for bread crumbs – meaning stale bread that has been processed in the blender until crumbs form. These are vastly superior to the store-bought variety!

1 cup chopped onion (about ½ medium onion)
¹/₃ cup chopped green bell pepper (about ½ medium bell pepper)
1 tablespoon plus 1 teaspoon kosher salt
1 tablespoon freshly ground black pepper
1 tablespoon dried oregano

1 tablespoon fennel seed, toasted and finely chopped (or ground in a spice grinder)
1 tablespoon minced fresh thyme
1 tablespoon minced fresh rosemary
2 teaspoons minced garlic (about 2 medium garlic cloves)
1 teaspoon red pepper flakes
½ cup heavy cream
1 large egg
2 cups bread crumbs
1 pound ground pork
1 pound ground beef

Preheat oven to 400 degrees.

Combine onion, bell pepper, salt, black pepper, oregano, fennel, thyme, rosemary, garlic, and red pepper flakes in a blender or food processor; puree. Add cream and egg; pulse to combine. Transfer mixture to a large bowl. Add bread crumbs; stir until well combined.

Combine ground pork and beef in a large bowl; work together with hands until just combined. Add pureed vegetable mixture; work together with hands until just combined (do not overwork!). Form into a loaf. Bake for 30 minutes at 400 degrees, until a nice crust forms. Lower oven to 325 degrees and cook for about 45 minutes longer, until an internal thermometer reads 160 degrees. Allow to rest for 5 minutes. Slice and serve over mashed potatoes or grits. (See recipe for mashed potatoes on page 110 and recipe for grits on page 102).

YIELD: About 6 servings

P.S. Leftovers make delicious sandwiches!

TOMATO SAUCE
1 tablespoon vegetable oil
1 cup chopped onion (about ½ medium onion)
½ cup chopped green bell pepper (about ½
    medium bell pepper)
1 tablespoon dark brown sugar
1 teaspoon kosher salt
1 teaspoon freshly ground black pepper
2 teaspoons minced garlic (about 2 medium garlic
    cloves)
1 12-ounce beer (of your choice!)
1 28-ounce can crushed tomatoes
½ cup ketchup
1 tablespoon Worcestershire sauce
1 tablespoon tomato paste

Heat oil in a medium pot over medium heat. Add
onion, bell pepper, sugar, salt, and black pepper.
Saute until onions are translucent, about 10 minutes.
Add garlic and cook until fragrant, about 30 seconds. Add beer; stir to combine, loosening any bits
that have collected in bottom of pan. Add tomatoes,
ketchup, Worcestershire, and tomato paste. Simmer,
stirring occasionally. Cook until reduced by half and
a nice thick sauce has formed, about 30 minutes.

YIELD: About 1 quart

Cathy's Country Fried Steak

My partner Chris's mother, Cathy, found the basis for her country fried steak recipe in a cookbook given to her as a wedding present. Over the years, she turned it into her own creation, and both her children loved this special treat. They would always request it for their birthday dinners, and they still gush when they talk about it today. Chris added a bit of chef's finesse to his mother's masterpiece, but he certainly did not mess with the Saltine cracker crust.

4 cubed steaks, about ⅓ pound each
3 teaspoons kosher salt
3 teaspoons freshly ground black pepper
½ cup plus 2 tablespoons all-purpose flour
¼ cup milk
2 large eggs
2 cups Saltine crackers, crushed (1 sleeve of crackers)
¼ cup vegetable oil, plus more if needed
2 cups chopped onion (about 1 medium onion)
1 teaspoon minced garlic (about 1 medium garlic clove)
2 cups chicken stock, or canned low-sodium chicken broth
2 tablespoons heavy cream

Preheat oven to 250 degrees.

In a shallow bowl or baking dish, season meat with 1½ teaspoons salt and 1½ teaspoons pepper; set aside.

Combine ½ cup flour, 1 teaspoon salt, and 1 teaspoon pepper in another shallow dish; set aside.Whisk together milk and eggs in a large bowl; set aside. Crush Saltines in another shallow dish; set aside. Dredge each steak in the flour mixture, then in the milk-egg mixture, and finally through the crushed Saltines. Transfer to a plate or baking dish and reserve.

Heat oil in a large skillet over medium-low heat. Add steaks and cook until well browned, about 8 minutes per side. Remove each steak to a paper towel-lined plate. Hold in oven to keep warm. (Depending on the size of your pan and the size of your steaks, you will most likely need to cook the steaks 2 at a time. If necessary, add more oil to the pan before cooking your second batch.)

If no oil remains after cooking steaks, add another 2 tablespoons vegetable oil. Then add onions, remaining ½ teaspoon salt, and remaining ½ teaspoon pepper; cook, stirring regularly, until onions are translucent, about 10 minutes. Add garlic and cook until fragrant, about 30 seconds. Add remaining 2 tablespoons flour; cook, stirring constantly, until your roux has become a light blonde color, 2 to 3 minutes. Add stock and cook until reduced by ¾, about 15 minutes. At this point, your sauce should be relatively thick – an appropriate gravy consistency. Add heavy cream and bring to a simmer. Cook, stirring, until mixture comes together into a creamy gravy, about 1 minute. Remove from heat and reserve.

Remove steaks from oven and serve with gravy ladled over them. Serve with rice or mashed potatoes (see recipe on page 110).

YIELD: 4 servings

Chuck's Italian Sausage Ragout

We call this an Italian Sausage Ragout, but really it's my partner's take on Bolognese, the classic northern Italian pasta sauce. Traditionally, it is tossed with fresh tagliatelle, but at the GO, we serve it with our house-made handkerchief pasta or locally made cavatelli. If you happen to enjoy making fresh pasta yourself, or can buy some, I would highly recommend taking that extra step, but even dried noodles produce an outstanding meal.

1 28-ounce can whole peeled tomatoes
½ cup finely chopped bacon (about 5 ounces or 4 to 5 standard grocery store slices)
1 pound ground pork butt
1 tablespoon toasted fennel seed, finely chopped or ground in spice grinder
1 tablespoon dried oregano
2 teaspoons kosher salt
1 teaspoon freshly ground black pepper
½ teaspoon red pepper flakes
1 cup chopped onion (about ½ medium onion)
½ cup chopped carrot (about 1 medium carrot)
½ cup chopped celery (about 1½ stalks)
2 teaspoons minced garlic (about 2 medium garlic cloves)
¾ cup heavy cream
½ cup chicken stock or canned low-sodium chicken broth
¼ cup tomato paste
½ cup chicken livers, pureed in blender or food processor or finely chopped

1 pound cooked pasta (of your choice)
Parmesan cheese, for garnish

In a large bowl break apart tomatoes with your hands; set aside.

Heat a large pot over medium heat. Add the bacon and cook until browned, 5 to 10 minutes. Add ground pork, fennel, oregano, salt, black pepper, and red pepper flakes. Cook, stirring constantly so that pork does not clump, for another 5 minutes. Add onions, carrot, and celery and cook until onions are trans-lucent, about 10 minutes. Add garlic and cook until fragrant, another 30 seconds. Add tomatoes, cream, stock, and tomato paste; stir to combine.

Simmer until about 75 percent of liquid has cooked down, about 45 minutes.

Add livers and cook another 5 minutes. Remove from heat and allow to rest for another 5 minutes before tossing with pasta. Garnish with freshly grated Parmesan cheese.

YIELD: 6 to 8 servings

P.S. Don't be scared off by the chicken livers that finish this dish. They add a necessary richness, but most folks would never place the flavor. They can be your "secret" ingredient!

Bologna

Aunt E's Pot Roast

As a young line cook, my partner Charles lived with his Aunt Elizabeth in uptown New Orleans, and often she would leave dinner out for him. This pot roast became his favorite, as he would slice it and make a decadent sandwich. At the GO, we used this as inspiration for our own pot roast po boy, but we also serve it over mashed potatoes, as seen here.

3½- to 4-pound boneless chuck roast, tied
4 small garlic cloves, quartered
2½ tablespoons kosher salt
2 tablespoons freshly ground black pepper
All-purpose flour for dusting
¼ cup vegetable oil
4 cups chopped onions (about 2 medium onions)
¼ cup red wine
2 quarts canned low-sodium beef broth
About 20 sprigs of fresh thyme, tied in a bundle with
    kitchen twine
1 sprig of fresh rosemary
2 bay leaves
2 cups roughly chopped carrots (about 4 medium
    carrots)

Preheat the oven to 350 degrees.

Pat the beef dry with a paper towel. Using a paring knife, cut 16 thin slits, evenly spaced, in the beef. Stick the pieces of garlic down into these slits (this is called "studding"). Season the beef with 1½ tablespoons salt and 1 tablespoon pepper. Dredge the whole roast in flour, including the ends. In a large Dutch oven or other large pot, heat 2 tablespoons vegetable oil over medium heat. Add the roast and sear for 4 to 5 minutes on each side, until nicely browned. Transfer the roast to a baking dish.

Add the remaining 2 tablespoons vegetable oil to the Dutch oven. Add the onions, remaining 1 tablespoon of salt, and remaining 1 tablespoon of pepper and cook, stirring occasionally, until translucent, about 10 minutes. Add wine and stir vigorously to release any bits of goodness that have collected at the bottom of the pot. Add the beef broth, thyme, rosemary, and bay leaves; stir to combine. Add the reserved roast and bring to a simmer. Cover and bake in the oven for 3 hours. Add the carrots and bake until meat is very tender (begins to shred when prodded with a fork), about 1 more hour.

Carefully remove the pot from the oven and transfer the roast to a cutting board. Remove the strings from the roast and gently slice the meat. Serve slices over mashed potatoes (see recipe on page 110) with some of the vegetables and cooking liquid.

Discard thyme, rosemary, and bay leaves before serving.

YIELD: About 6 servings

P.S. In keeping with Aunt Elizabeth's style, we offer up this very traditional pot roast recipe, but feel free to fancy yours up with the addition of parsnips, turnips, mushrooms, or other appropriate vegetables. These could be added alongside the carrots (towards the end of cooking) to ensure that they are tender but not mushy.

Chicken and Sausage Jambalaya

Jambalaya is a classic dish of south Louisiana, which should come as no surprise, given the amount of rice grown in the region. While some prospered from the crop, others struggled both in New Orleans and in the countryside southwest of the city. Thus, rice gave birth to a culture built upon making a little bit go a long way; jambalaya is the epitome of this philosophy. You will find jambalayas made with anything from rabbit to duck. Here we keep ours pretty basic with roasted chicken and andouille sausage. Andouille is a staple of Louisiana cooking and can be mail ordered from the folks who actually make it (visit www.poches.com) – or another high-quality smoked sausage can be substituted.

And if you find yourself short on time, simply buy a roasted chicken from the grocery rather than roasting your own. You'll find yourself with a enough food for a party in just over an hour!

5 tablespoons unsalted butter
2 pounds diced andouille sausage, or other smoked
    sausage
3 cups chopped onion (about 1½ medium onions)
2 cups chopped celery (about 6 stalks)
2 cups chopped green bell pepper (about 2½ medium
    bell peppers)
1 tablespoon kosher salt
2 teaspoons freshly ground black pepper
1 tablespoon minced garlic (about 3 medium cloves)
1 brined and roasted 4- to 5- pound chicken (see
    recipe page 10) (about 4½ cups pulled chicken)

1 quart chicken stock or canned low-sodium chicken broth
1 28-ounce can crushed tomatoes
About 20 sprigs of fresh thyme, tied in a bundle with kitchen twine
2 bay leaves
3 tablespoons hot sauce
1 tablespoon Worcestershire sauce
2 teaspoons ground coriander
1 quart Uncle Ben's rice, or other parboiled rice
½ cup chopped green onions (about 6 green onions)

Preheat oven to 450 degrees.

In a large pot, melt butter over medium-high heat. Add andouille. Cook until lightly browned, 5 to 10 minutes, stirring occasionally. Add onions, celery, bell pepper, salt, and pepper and cook until onions are translucent, about 10 minutes. Add garlic and cook until fragrant, about 30 seconds. Add pulled meat from roasted chicken, chicken stock, tomatoes, thyme, bay leaves, hot sauce, Worcestershire, and coriander; stir to combine. When it comes up to a simmer, add rice, cover with a tight-fitting lid, and put in oven. Cook for 40 minutes to an hour, until rice has absorbed all of the liquid and is tender. (Do not check before 40 minutes, as you will interrupt the steaming process.)

Remove from oven. Discard thyme bundle and bay leaves. Add green onions; stir to thoroughly combine. Serve immediately, as the rice will continue to cook in the lidded pot. Alternatively, transfer rice to another serving vessel until ready to serve.

Serve with hot sauce.

Yield: About 12 servings

P.S. You will notice a wide range on the final cooking time for this dish. This depends largely how tightly your pot's lid fits and consequently its ability to retain steam. The rice should be moist but not wet with excess liquid.

Country Captain

I have to admit that as a child, I was not a fan of
Country Captain. Its ubiquitous presence at any
gathering requiring a covered dish and its "exotic"
flavors did not enamor me. But my family's strong
allegiance to the dish finally won me over. They claim
it originated in my hometown of Columbus, Georgia
and was much requested by dignitaries ranging from
General Patton to President Franklin Roosevelt. Lord
knows where the truth lies, but they passed down a
much rougher version of this recipe for generations. I
have honed it a bit myself, and at the GO, we have
restaurantified it down to simply a chicken breast.
Here you will find the perfect home version using a
whole chicken. It yields dinner for two with plenty
of leftovers or dinner for four, if some folks are happy
eating dark meat.

1½ cups all-purpose flour
2 teaspoons kosher salt
1 teaspoon freshly ground black pepper
1 whole chicken, rinsed and cut into 8 pieces
3 tablespoons vegetable oil
2 tablespoons unsalted butter
1 cup chopped yellow onion (about ½ medium
    onion)
1 cup chopped green bell pepper (about 1 large
    bell pepper)
½ cup chopped celery (about 1½ medium stalks)
2 tablespoons yellow curry powder
2 cloves of garlic, thinly sliced
1 bay leaf
2 28-ounce cans crushed tomatoes

1 cup chicken stock
1 tablespoon hot sauce
1 tablespoon Worcestershire sauce
1 tablespoon light brown sugar
1 tablespoon tomato paste
20 sprigs of fresh thyme, tied in a bundle with kitchen twine
½ cup raisins
½ cup sliced toasted almonds

Combine flour, 1 teaspoon salt, and pepper in a large shallow dish; stir to blend. Dredge the chicken pieces in the flour mixture, coating evenly. Shake off any excess. Set aside.

Heat the oil and 1 tablespoon butter in a large pot over medium-high heat. Cook the chicken, in batches, until lightly browned, 3 to 4 minutes per side. Transfer the chicken to paper towels to drain; set aside.

Add the remaining tablespoon butter to the saucepan and add the onions, bell peppers, celery, curry powder, garlic, bay leaf, and remaining teaspoon of salt. Cook, stirring, until the onions are translucent, about 10 minutes.

Add the tomatoes, chicken stock, hot sauce, Worcestershire, brown sugar, tomato paste, and thyme. Stir to blend, bring to a simmer, and then reduce the heat to medium. Add the chicken and cook, stirring occasionally, until very tender but not falling off the bones, about 50 minutes. Add the raisins and cook until plump, about 10 minutes longer.

Discard thyme bundle and bay leaf. Serve hot over steamed white rice. Garnish with the almonds.

Yield: 2 to 4 servings

P.S. This recipe can easily be doubled if you are having a small dinner party. It is terrific party fare!

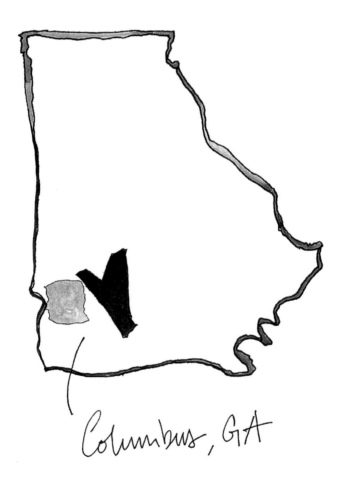

Columbus, GA

Buttermilk Fried Chicken

There is just something about fried chicken that reaches out across all ages and cultures. At the GO, we serve it only on Tuesday nights, and this is truly a special occasion. We believe that ours is extra special because we use all-natural chickens. These days it is not overly difficult or expensive to find such birds, and we swear you can taste the difference.

Vegetable oil for frying
1 buttermilk-brined chicken (see recipe below)
2 cups self-rising flour
2 cups all-purpose flour
1½ tablespoons kosher salt
1 tablespoon freshly ground black pepper
1 tablespoon freshly ground white pepper
1 teaspoon cayenne

Heat 4 inches of oil to 325 degrees in a large pot.

Combine self-rising flour, all-purpose flour, salt, black pepper, white pepper, and cayenne in a brown paper grocery bag. (Two bags – one inside the other – ensures no blowouts!)

Remove the chicken from the buttermilk and shake to remove excess. Add the chicken in batches to the flour mixture (in the bag) and shake to completely coat. Remove and shake over trash can to remove excess flour. (Alternatively, you could simply combine the flour/seasoning in a shallow baking dish and dredge the chicken pieces through it. However, the paper bag method thoroughly coats the chicken and, in my opinion, happens to be more fun!)

Place on a wire rack set over a baking sheet to rest until ready to fry, at least 30 minutes. (Allowing the chicken to rest after flouring ensures that the flour will better adhere to the chicken during the frying process.)

Fry the chicken in batches, skin-side down, until golden brown, about 8 minutes. Turn and fry until golden brown on the second side and cooked through, about 8 minutes longer. Remove and drain on paper towel-lined sheet pan.

An instant-read thermometer should read 165 degrees when chicken is probed. If your chicken happens to be slightly under, you can finish it in the oven at 350 degrees.

YIELD: 4 to 6 servings

P.S. Don't be intimidated by this recipe – just allow yourself time to brine and time to fry. The good thing about fried chicken is that it tastes really good at room temperature. So unlike fried seafood, you could do all the work in advance and sit down to enjoy the feast with your friends/family without forsaking flavor!

P.P.S. An even oil temperature is key to frying at home. A clip-on candy/fry thermometer should be kept in the pot at all times, and the temperature should register at least 300 degrees during the frying process.

BUTTERMILK BRINED CHICKEN
1 quart buttermilk
¼ cup hot sauce
¼ cup kosher salt
2 teaspoons minced garlic (about 1 large garlic clove)
2 teaspoons freshly ground black pepper
1 teaspoon cayenne
1 whole chicken rinsed and cut into 8 serving pieces

Combine buttermilk, hot sauce, salt, garlic, pepper, and cayenne in a large bowl; stir to combine. Add chicken pieces and make sure all are submerged. Cover and refrigerate for 24 hours.

Allan Benton

Allan Benton – The King of Bacon

Allan Benton has achieved celebrity status in the world of food, but you wouldn't know it talking to him. He speaks with that honest-to-goodness modesty I associate with folks who really grew up in the country.

Allan grew up so far out "you had to look straight up to see daylight," and that's where he learned the art of curing his now-famous bacon and ham.

His birth certificate doesn't list a city, just Scott County, Virginia. Allan split his childhood between this area of southern Virginia and northern Tennessee, where he now resides. His parents' families homesteaded adjoining plots in Virginia, and Allan spent much time there, learning the art of working the land from his grandparents.

"Do you remember that television show 'The Waltons'?" he asks. "Well, we made the Waltons look like they lived in town."

Allan's grandparents did not own cars or tractors. They walked where they needed to go and worked the land using a mule. They raised heirloom varieties of vegetables because they could not afford to buy seeds. They grew their crops organically because they could not afford to buy commercial fertilizer. And they let their hogs forage for acorns because they could not afford to buy grain.

On Thanksgiving day, they woke before dawn to butcher these 500- to 700-pound hogs, putting every part to use. "We either canned it, cured it, or ground it into sausage," says Allan.

"Looking back now, I realize it was the depths of south Appalachian poverty, but it was an incredible way of life," he says.

He took the lessons he learned there and held them close, even as he went on to college and graduate school in Tennessee. After earning his masters in 1973, Allan sat down and looked at the salary schedule for his future as a guidance counselor.

"I realized I might have made a poor career choice," he says with a laugh.

About this same time and in the same county, Albert Hicks decided to sell his country ham business, and fate took a crucial turn. Allan heard of the sale and made a gamble. He began leasing the primitive operation from Albert. He amassed information from food science professors, Albert, and his own childhood; and thus he began curing pork bellies and hams.

"For the first 20 years I thought we might starve to death," he says, once again with a laugh.

He remembers that one day his father walked in the store and asked, "How much money do you think you've made this year?"

"I didn't know," says Allan.

His father kept his books at this time and broke it to him, "Well, I can tell you – you haven't made a dime!"

At his father's insistence Allan raised his prices, and he eventually moved the operation to where it resides today on Highway 411, still in Monroe County. Here, he attracted more customers and gained his Federal Department of Agriculture (FDA) certification.

Finally in the early 90s, Blackberry Farm – a rural Tennessee resort, began using his product – and their chef, John Fleer, spread the gospel of Benton's Country Hams. Word of his superior bacon and hams soon made its way to celebrity chefs on both coasts, and orders increased to a point that finally gave the Benton family some security.

Now, Allan cures nearly twice as many hams and 20 times as many bellies as he did at the outset. He estimates that 400 restaurants mail order from him – about 40 of those are in New York City and about 50 are in California.

Allan, in his usual modesty, credits much of this success to that first support from John Fleer and Blackberry Farm. He also credits his forefathers.

"I'm not speeding up the process like a lot of folks," he says. "I don't take to change well."

He continues to use his original family recipe of salt, brown sugar, black, and red pepper for any ham aged 12 months or longer – just as he continues to use a rotary dial phone in his cinderblock storefront.

Allan does admit to one change: now he purchases exclusively all-natural, heritage pork. Over the years, he witnessed a drastic transformation in commercially raised hogs, as they became leaner and leaner.

"I grew up eating incredible pork," he says. "I knew what pork was supposed to taste like."

Now, he buys the older breeds of hogs that have better marbling and flavor from coops around the country.

"You have to start with something good to make something good," Allan says. And that's his primary aim: excellence.

"My goal is to make something as good as Europe or anywhere else," he says.

* * *

At the Glass Onion, we believe Allan Benton achieves his ambition handily. While testing recipes for the cookbook, I found results to be drastically different when I substituted another high-quality bacon. There is a sweet smokiness to his product that casts a spell over a dish. He believes that chefs elevate his products, but we believe that he elevates our food.

Bubba Craven with Mark and Annie Filion

Keegan-Filion – Whole Hog Farming

Seems like Mark and Annie Filion just could not escape farming. Mark's grandfather raised chickens in Rhode Island, and Annie's grandfather farmed the Walterboro, SC property that they now call Keegan-Filion Farm. On this land they raise free-range chickens and hogs – both sought after by Charleston chefs.

But, of course, their story does not wrap up quite so neatly. Their current operation began in 2004; yet, Mark and Annie first tried their hand at farming in 1986, raising commercial hogs for Smithfield. As the demand for such "factory pork" grew, smaller farmers like the Filions became priced out of the game. In 1994 they sold their remaining hogs and began leasing the land to other local farmers. Mark focused his attention on his "day job" as a sales manager for a pipe valve company, and Annie became a purchasing agent at a Walterboro plant.

Ten years later, Annie found herself working 50 to 60 hours a week and not getting anywhere. She wanted to do work that would benefit the community; so, the Filions sat down and came up with a couple of options. They debated between creating a taxi service for the elderly or starting an organic market, and in 2004, they opened The Farm Store right outside their front door. There, they sold all-natural produce purchased from a large distribution company out of Florida. They had moderate success at the beginning, but soon larger grocery stores and even Walmart began carrying some organics, which obviously hurt the demand for their small operation.

Luckily, the Filions had a fallback plan, whether they realized it or not. Concurrently with opening the market, they had once again begun to work their land. Over the past decade they had watched tenants basically destroy the property with bad farming practices, and they knew they had a long road ahead of them. First, they bought laying hens. This seemed a manageable project and a good way to rehabilitate the soil. Next came broiler chickens and finally hogs at the request of several Charleston chefs. The Filions had their doubts about entering the hog business again, but they moved ahead, determined to do it differently this time. They enlisted their good friend Bubba Craven as a business partner and began breeding a heritage line known as Tamworth.

The Fillions sold their first hog to Chef Craig Diehl (of Cypress restaurant) in 2007, and they both delivered the finished product to him with a bit of anxiety, worried he might not like their pork. They stood by as Chef Diehl began cutting chops, and Mark remembers his murmuring, "Oh...oh....oh..." Then Chef Diehl turned to them and said, "This is fantastic!"

The marbling of the Filions' pork has since become near legendary, and they really cannot keep up with the demand for their hogs or chickens. While this might sound like unequivocal success, the Filions still struggle. Producing superior flavor takes time, and, of course, time means money.

So, Mark continues to work his "day job"; now he manages industrial sales for another corporate entity. Basically, he spends his weeks on the road and his weekends on the farm. Annie works the farm with the full-time help of Bubba and a few other part-time employees, delivering to Charleston restaurants once a week and visiting the processing facility in Kingstree once every two weeks. All of this adds up to countless hours of labor and very little time together, but the Filions still deem it worthwhile. Every Saturday evening they go to church and then have dinner with Mark's mother at the local Greek restaurant, and for now maybe that's enough.

Of course, one day, Mark hopes to farm full time and possibly bring their son Jessie into the family business. But all in all, he seems satisfied and surprisingly unstressed.

"What we do is not any different than anyone else, except we also have about 4,000 animals that depend on us," he says without a bit of irony.

* * *

At the GO, we feel especially proud when Annie delivers a whole hog. We use every bit – making everything from breakfast sausage to pate out of this delectable pork.

CHAPTER 4

Sides

Housemade Pickles

My partner Chris refers to these as "Holy Crap! Those Are Good Pickles." The pickles really are outstanding, and on top of that, they are super easy to make. You should make these all summer long when local cucumbers are dirt cheap and delicious. At the GO, we serve them as a side, and we also puree them for homemade pickle relish. They have just the perfect amount of sweetness to seduce the palate without overwhelming it.

5 medium cucumbers, peeled on 3 sides and sliced
   ¾ inch thick
½ medium sweet onion, thinly sliced
½ medium red bell pepper, thinly sliced
1 small carrot, peeled and thinly sliced into rounds
½ cup kosher salt
4 cups cider vinegar
4 cups sugar
1 teaspoon black peppercorns
1 teaspoon mustard seed
½ teaspoon celery seed
½ teaspoon red pepper flakes

Combine cucumbers, onion, bell pepper, carrot, and salt in a large bowl or storage container. Let sit for one hour. Rinse thoroughly with cold water. Return to a large bowl or storage container.

Combine remaining ingredients in a large pot and bring to a boil. Pour liquid over vegetables, cover, and refrigerate. Refrigerate overnight before serving.

YIELD: About 2 quarts

Cole Slaw

A Southern cookbook would not be complete without a recipe for cole slaw. It is a necessary accoutrement to so many good things – fried catfish, fried chicken...

Our version is straightforward and meant to complement rather than compete with the centerpiece of your meal!

1 head of green cabbage
1 serving slaw sauce (see recipe below)
½ cup plus 1 tablespoon sweet pickle relish
¼ cup plus 2 tablespoons chopped green onions
1 tablespoon kosher salt
2 teaspoons freshly ground black pepper

Remove outer leaves from cabbage. Cut into quarters and cut out core. Cut each quarter in half crosswise and then thinly slice each of these chunks lengthwise.

Combine all ingredients in a large bowl and toss to combine. Cover and refrigerate overnight.

Yield: 8 to 10 servings; about 2 quarts

SLAW SAUCE
1 cup plus 3 tablespoons mayonnaise
¼ cup plus 2 tablespoons cider vinegar
1 tablespoon sugar
1 tablespoon honey
½ teaspoon hot sauce

Combine all ingredients in a medium bowl; whisk to combine.

P.S. The slicing directions might seem a bit complicated, but we are trying to ensure you end up with easy-to-eat pieces of cabbage. At the restaurant, we use an electric slicer, which makes things simpler! But this method should yield a relatively fine slaw.

P.P.S. You can go totally GO and make your sweet pickle relish from our Housemade Pickles recipe (see recipe on page 96). Simply drain the pickles and pulse them in a food processor or blender until they are roughly pureed.

Potato Salad

Some might call us crazy, but we only make our potato salad when beautiful, local potatoes happen to be in season. Consequently, we don't gussy our recipe up too much. The deliciousness comes from the flavor of the potatoes.

1 quart diced red or white potatoes (not Russets)
    (about 16 small potatoes)
1 tablespoon plus ½ teaspoon kosher salt
¹/₃ cup mayonnaise
¼ cup chopped onion
¼ cup sweet pickle relish
2 tablespoons sour cream
1 teaspoon freshly ground black pepper

Place potatoes in a large pot. Cover with water. Add 1 tablespoon of salt. Bring to a boil and cook until tender, about 5 minutes. Drain and allow to cool.

Combine with remaining ingredients in a large bowl; toss to combine. Season with remaining ½ teaspoon of salt. Cover and refrigerate.

Yield: 4 to 6 servings; about 1 quart

P.S. You can go totally GO and make your sweet pickle relish from our Housemade Pickles recipe (see recipe on page 96). Simply drain the pickles and pulse them in a food processor or blender until they are roughly pureed.

Anson Mills Grits

We give full credit for the tastiness of our grits to Anson Mills. Founder Glenn Roberts has made it his mission to bring back heirloom varieties of grains because of their superior flavor, and his grits certainly prove the worthiness of his mission. These are simply amazing grits. You can order them yourself from www.ansonmills. com – along with other heritage grains. We use the "quick" variety, as we prefer their finer texture and shorter cooking time.

Glenn often stops by the GO when he is in Charleston visiting his daughter Ansley. They enjoy one of our staple plates that features his grits – Crispy Braised Pork Belly with Grits and Greens.

Read Glenn's story on page 117.

¼ pound (1 stick) unsalted butter
2 cups Anson Mills "Carolina Whole Hominy Quick Yellow Grits"
2 cups heavy cream
1 tablespoon kosher salt
2 teaspoons freshly ground black pepper

Combine 5 cups water with butter in a medium pot over medium heat. Bring to a boil. Slowly add grits, stirring continuously. Reduce to a simmer and cook, stirring occasionally, until tender, about 1 hour. As the grits cook, they will absorb water and become some-what thick. Add cream in increments to prevent grits thickening to an unyielding mass. More water can also be added as necessary to yield to your preferred consistency. Season with salt and pepper.

YIELD: 8 to 10 servings; about 2 quarts

P.S. If you happen to live in the Charleston area, you can buy these grits directly from the GO!

Sea Island Red Peas

Yes, to make these peas you will have to order them from www.ansonmills.com, but they will be well worth the effort. Anson Mills recently helped to bring this heirloom variety of field pea back into broader production. Sea Island Red Peas originated in Africa but came to the coastal Carolina area with slaves in the early 18th century. Traditionally, they were eaten alongside rice, and almost every Sea Island kitchen garden had a crop of peas. Some of the most interesting Sea Island Red Peas "rediscovered" by Anson Mills came from Robert Johnson, a retired sheriff in the ACE Basin, who donated his grandmother's peas after she passed.

At the GO, we rely on Sea Island Red Peas in the winter when fresh field peas are not available; their earthy flavor proves the perfect accompaniment to cold weather. And we highly recommend eating them on New Year's Day for good luck!

14 ounces Sea Island Red Peas, rinsed
1 quart chicken stock or canned low-sodium chicken broth
2 tablespoons vegetable oil
2 cups chopped onion (about 1 medium onion)
¾ cup chopped green bell pepper (about 1 medium bell pepper)
¾ cup chopped celery (about 3 medium celery stalks)
1 tablespoon sliced garlic (about 2 medium garlic cloves)
1 teaspoon freshly ground black pepper

½ teaspoon freshly ground white pepper
1 teaspoon dried oregano
Pinch of red pepper flakes
About 20 sprigs of fresh thyme, tied in a bundle with
    kitchen twine
1 bay leaf
1 smoked ham hock
1 teaspoon kosher salt

Combine peas and 2 cups chicken stock in a medium
bowl. Cover and refrigerate overnight.

Heat oil in a medium pot over medium heat. Add
onion, bell pepper, celery, and garlic. Cook, stirring
occasionally, until onions are translucent, about
10 minutes. Add black pepper, white pepper, oregano, and red pepper flakes; stir to combine. Add
peas and their soaking liquid; stir to combine. Add
remaining 2 cups stock, thyme, bay leaf, and ham
hock. Bring to a boil. Reduce to a simmer and cook
until peas are tender, about 1½ hours. Add enough
stock or water to keep peas covered during cooking
process. Season with salt.

Discard thyme bundle and bay
leaf before serving.

YIELD: 8 to 10 servings; about 2
quarts

P.S. Do not add salt until the end of
cooking peas or beans to ensure
that they do not split open.

Creamed Corn

Like our Chilled Corn Soup, this recipe should really be made at the height of corn season. Down South, that would be around July. Toward the end of summer, the corn loses its sweetness and becomes a bit tough. But under prime conditions, this creamed corn should knock your socks off!

5 ears of corn
1 medium onion, halved
About 20 sprigs of fresh thyme, tied in a bundle with kitchen twine
1 bay leaf
¼ cup chopped bacon (about 2 ounces or 2 standard grocery store slices)
2 teaspoons kosher salt
1 teaspoon freshly ground black pepper
2 tablespoons all-purpose flour
2 tablespoons heavy cream
1 teaspoon honey, optional

Cut corn kernels from cob and reserve. Combine corn cobs, half of the onion, thyme, and bay leaf in a large pot. Cover with water, about 12 cups. Bring to a boil, reduce to a simmer, and cook for 1 hour. (The 12 cups of water should reduce down to about 6 cups of "corn water.") Remove from the heat and strain through a colander into a large bowl. Reserve "corn water" for later use.

Chop remaining half of the onion. Saute bacon in a medium pot over medium heat until browned, about 5 minutes. Add onion, 1 teaspoon salt, and pepper;

cook until onion is translucent, about 10 minutes. Add flour and stir to combine. Add all of reserved "corn water," corn kernels, cream, and remaining teaspoon of salt. Bring to a boil and then reduce to a simmer. Cook until reduced by about three-fourths, 1 to 1½ hours. Corn should dominate the liquid component. If corn needs a little extra sweetness, add the honey.

YIELD: 4 to 6 servings; about 1 quart

Braised Local Greens

In the South, there's just no escaping braised greens! Collard greens, turnip greens, mustard greens – they are like the life force of the region. At the GO, we mostly cook collards, and we prepare them in a fairly traditional way – start with some pork fat and onion, simmer, and voila! We do use a fair amount of vinegar in ours so that you might not even need to serve them with the precursory condiment of pepper vinegar, but you be the judge.

¾ cup chopped bacon (about 7 ounces or 6 standard grocery store slices)
2 to 3 pounds cleaned and cut collards (about 1 gallon once cut and cleaned; see instructions below)
2 cups sliced onion (about 1 medium onion)
1 tablespoon kosher salt
2 teaspoons freshly ground black pepper
2 teaspoons minced garlic (about 2 medium garlic cloves)
¼ cup cider vinegar
1 tablespoon light brown sugar
2 teaspoons hot sauce

First, a note on cleaning and cutting greens. Washing your greens is of utmost importance because, often times, they can be extremely sandy. If yours do not seem especially dirty, you can try simply washing the individual leaves under cold running water. But if your greens are straight from the field, you might need to fill the largest vessel in your kitchen with cold water and dunk your greens in – giving them a good swim. Once your greens are washed, simply cut out the thick spine running up the middle. Then lay the de-stemmed leaves on top of each other and slice, yielding a nice, bite-sized rectangle (you might also think of this as a thick julienne cut). Now you are ready to cook some greens!

Heat a large pot over a medium-high heat. Add bacon and cook until browned, about 10 minutes. Reduce heat to medium; add onion, salt, and pepper and cook until onions are translucent, about 10 minutes. Add garlic and cook until fragrant, about 30 seconds. Add vinegar, brown sugar, and hot sauce; stir to combine. Add greens and 4 quarts of water; stir to combine. Bring to a simmer and cook until greens are tender, about 2 hours.

YIELD: 8 to 10 servings; about 2 quarts

P.S. In a recipe like this that relies heavily on the flavor of bacon, a lot will depend on the quality/salt content of the bacon you use. At the GO, we use Allan Benton's bacon (read his story on page 85), which imparts a lot of smoke and salt (i.e., flavor) into our greens. We highly recommend using an artisanal bacon like this; otherwise, you might need to increase your seasoning.

Mashed Potatoes

Most folks probably feel they have their very own mashed potato technique hammered down, but I know we can teach you at least one trick with the GO recipe. The trick lies in drying out the potatoes after they are boiled but before mashing them. Drawing out the moisture ensures uber-rich mashed potatoes. The butter and cream don't hurt either!

5 medium Russet potatoes, peeled
½ cup plus 1 teaspoon kosher salt
2 cups heavy cream
½ pound (2 sticks) unsalted butter
About 20 sprigs of fresh thyme
2 garlic cloves, crushed
1 bay leaf
2 teaspoons freshly ground white pepper

Preheat oven to 400 degrees.

Combine potatoes and ½ cup salt in a large pot of water. Bring to a boil. Cook until tender, about 30 minutes once boiling.

Remove potatoes from water and place on a baking sheet. Bake until slightly dried out, 5 to 10 minutes. Remove from oven and place in a large bowl.

Combine cream, butter, thyme, garlic, and bay leaf in a medium pot over medium heat. Bring to a simmer. Pour mixture through a fine-meshed strainer into the bowl of potatoes. Work vigorously with a whisk. Whip until relatively smooth and all ingredients are incorporated. Season with white pepper and remaining 1 teaspoon salt.

Yield: 8 to 10 servings; about 2 quarts

P.S. As listed, we use Russet potatoes, but Yukon Golds also work nicely!

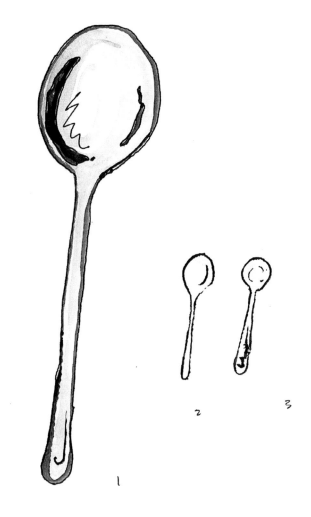

Cornbread

Ask a Southerner their preference on cornbread, and you are likely to receive an extensive monologue debating cornmeal, sugar, and more. We styled our cornbread with this in mind – trying to achieve a middle ground in density and sweetness. We highly recommend serving it with high-quality, local honey as a garnish.

Softened butter, for pan
1 cup yellow cornmeal
1 cup all-purpose flour
1 tablespoon salt
2 teaspoons baking powder
2 teaspoons sugar
2 large eggs
4 tablespoons (½ stick) unsalted butter, melted
2 cups buttermilk
Honey, for garnish

Preheat oven to 400 degrees.

Grease a 9-inch cast-iron skillet, or 8-inch square baking pan with softened butter. Whisk dry ingredients together in a large bowl; set aside. Whisk wet ingredients together in another large bowl. Pour wet ingredients into dry ingredients, stirring until just combined. Pour batter into pan and bake until a toothpick or knife inserted into center comes out clean, about one hour.

Allow to cool and then slice into wedges or squares, depending on your pan. Serve with honey.

Yield: 10 to 12 servings

Oyster Dressing

Although my partners and I grew up in different Southern states with varied culinary traditions, we all have fond memories of oyster dressing at Thanksgiving. We each had our different takes on the dish: one remembers pureed oysters; I remember a Saltine cracker topping. But here we took the best of all our memories and created an oyster dressing that we proudly sell at the GO for Thanksgiving pickup!

Softened butter, for pan
½ cup finely chopped bacon (about 4½ ounces or 4 standard grocery store slices)
2½ cups finely chopped onion (about 1 large onion)
1¼ cups finely chopped celery (about 3 medium stalks)
1 cup finely chopped carrot (about 1 medium carrot)
3 tablespoons thinly sliced garlic (about 3 garlic cloves)
1½ teaspoons kosher salt
1½ teaspoons freshly ground black pepper
1 recipe for Glass Onion Cornbread (see recipe on page 112), made at least one day in advance, crumbled (this recipe yields about 6 cups of crumbled cornbread)
1 pint oysters, liquor drained off and reserved
Chicken stock, enough that when combined with oyster liquor equals 2½ cups
¼ cup heavy cream
4 large eggs
1½ tablespoons finely chopped fresh sage
1½ tablespoons finely chopped fresh thyme

Preheat oven to 350 degrees.

Grease a 9-by-13-inch baking dish with softened butter.

Saute bacon in a large skillet over medium heat until crisp, about 5 minutes. Add onion, celery, carrot, and garlic to the skillet. Season with ½ teaspoon salt and ½ teaspoon pepper. Cook, stirring occasionally, until onions are translucent and all released liquid has cooked off, about 10 minutes. Remove from heat, transfer to large bowl and refrigerate until completely cool. Once cool, remove from refrigerator and add crumbled cornbread; stir to combine.

Combine oyster liquor, chicken stock, heavy cream, eggs, sage, thyme, and remaining teaspoon of salt and teaspoon of pepper in a medium bowl; whisk to combine. Add this mixture to cornbread-vegetable mixture and stir to combine. Add oysters and gently incorporate.

Pour dressing into baking dish. Bake until firm, about 1½ hours.

Yield: 10 to 12 servings

Glenn Roberts

Glenn Roberts – Father of Anson Mills

To understand the mind of artisanal grain guru Glenn Roberts, you must imagine a raging fire of knowledge. A quick conversation with him could jump from his mother's black-skillet cooking to moonshine to his cultivation of true benne. Do not be fooled by the seemingly random nature of these topics. Inside his mind, Glenn connects all sorts of ideas, just in a round-about way. Eventually, most wind back to his brain-child, Anson Mills, and the art of seed preservation.

Glenn officially founded Anson Mills in 1998 and began supplying heritage strands of rice and corn products to chefs around the country from his home base in Columbia, South Carolina. However, the cultivation of Anson Mills began long before that year, back before Glenn even considered farming as a career option. Glenn uses the word "nonlinear" to describe his professional track, and he does so with pride. "My idea was to be as counter intuitive as possible," he says.

Glenn was born in Delaware and raised in California, but his mother, Mary Elizabeth Clifton, has deep ties to the South. During the early 1900s her father owned hotels all along the eastern seaboard that catered to horse racing tracks. This afforded them a lodge near Savannah, a house on South Carolina's Edisto Island, and an African American cook and nanny who taught her the secrets of black-skillet cooking. In fact, she grew up pounding kitchen rice and hand-milling grits at their house on Edisto.

All of these lessons became exceedingly valuable when the Depression hit, and their family went from being comfortable to hoping they would not lose everything. Ultimately, Glenn's grandfather decided the best place for his daughter would be at the helm of their hotel in Aiken, South Carolina. Thus, she began running this property at age 14 in the depths of the Depression. "She was feeding more people out the back door than the front door," says Glenn. "Black and white – everyone was poor."

Eventually, his mother moved back to Delaware, and there she met his father. Their common love of music brought them together: he was the church choir director, and she was a talented vocalist. This passion ultimately led them to La Jolla, California, where they could study under the plethora of musicians that performed at the Hollywood Bowl.

Despite the move, Mary Elizabeth kept up her southern culinary ways, centered largely on rice. Glenn remembers that the cooking of rice was a ritual in their house that denoted a sense of honor. He also remembers, with a smile, that he was only allowed to cook rice for the dog. While Glenn treasures all of these kitchen memories now, at the time, he wanted nothing more than to be an astronaut. This never materialized, but he excelled in his studies and went to college at age 14 on a music and math scholarship. The college happened to be the University of North Carolina, and just like that his southern roots reconnected.

Glenn worked a myriad of jobs during college – none without purpose. As a doffer in a twine factory, he saw the power of primitive water-driven machinery. And as a musician he toured around the southeast extensively – experiencing firsthand the culture of the region his mother remembered fondly.

His major in topology – a branch of mathematics specializing in distorting an object's spacial properties – enabled him to break into the world of architecture upon graduation, and in this world he found his professional footing. He worked with one of the top firms at the time, and eventually developed hotel/restaurant design as his specialty. Glenn traveled up and down the Eastern seaboard resurrecting historic properties. He especially loved this line of work, as he loved working with chefs. He remembers that at the time, during the 1970s, there was a definite lack of locality in restaurant cuisine. The chefs that recognized this missing connection between farm and table happened to be those who came over from Europe to work at hotels.

"These great European chefs had walked away from a system of people [farmers] bringing stuff to their back doors," says Glenn.

Their interest in the agriculture behind the food lodged in Glenn's mind, right beside his mother's stories of freshly milled rice and grits. He had been sending her grits throughout his southern travels trying to satisfy her childhood memories, but she finally told him to stop wasting his time because they lacked any real flavor. "She wasn't trying to hurt anyone's feelings," says Glenn. "She just had a keen palate and remembered what they tasted like."

These thoughts came together just as Glenn approached burnout in the design world. He decided to take a break and chose Charleston as his retreat. He lived at the beach and found work on Junior Magwood's shrimp boat. Despite Glenn's desire to "do nothing" for a while, he gradually found himself

pulled into the Charleston food community. A redis-
covery of local foodways seemed to be underway,
and Glenn could not help but join the effort. He met
farmers like George and Celeste Albers and found
work at Perdita's restaurant. There, he cooked, but
perhaps more importantly, he developed relation-
ships with the largely African American staff who
had been there since 1952. "They remembered
everything from their grandparents... stuff that wasn't
normal uptown food in Charleston at the time," says
Glenn.

All of this simply added fuel to Glenn's fire. That
tiny flame lit by his mother began to burn brighter,
and before he knew it, Glenn found himself filled
with a burning desire to resurrect historic foodways –
specifically artisanal grains, and even more specifically, Carolina Gold Rice. Thankfully, he already
knew some of the key players like Dick and Tricia
Schulze who had repatriated Carolina Gold Rice on
their plantation near Savannah.

The Schulzes came by their seed through Texas
A&M University, and Glenn sought out seed there
as well. Luckily, he came away with not just seed
but also the acquaintances of a leading corn
and rice geneticist, Dr. Anna McClung, and a re-
nowned entomologist, Dr. Merle Shepherd. Both provided and continue to provide invaluable assistance
in his grain cultivation.

Finding the heirloom varieties of corn would require Glenn to dig a bit deeper in his past. He knew
that, sadly, corn had become one of America's most
industrialized crops and, consequently, an extremely homogenized crop. Many of the historic lines of
corn that possessed complex flavor and aroma also

happened to be difficult to grow. So the question became, "Who might still have corn seed that dated back before industrialized farming became such a dominant force?"

Glenn remembered from his days at the North Carolina twine factory that there had been much talk of bootleggers. The reality (legal or not) was that generations of rural southerners survived on their proficiency in distilling corn whiskey. This was a lifestyle that did not allow them to buy seed from the local co-op; but rather, they saved seeds from their crops year after year (going back decades). Through avenues that only Glenn could drum up, he found one such family that appreciated his interest in their agriculture and eventually grew a field of corn for him.

This first field of corn proved a valuable lesson for Glenn when a wind storm blew the entire crop down in a matter of minutes. The next year he grew smaller plots in multiple locations, and he finally yielded his first crop of corn. Of course, he sent some to his mother and took some back to the staff at Perdita's. The flavor brought back the memories that Glenn had sought out for so long.

Glenn specifically remembers when he finally succeeded in bringing his mother some freshly milled rice. "Quiet reflection over a bowl of rice is something to behold," he says.

Corn and rice proved just the beginning for Glenn; now he cultivates heritage wheat, peas, and more. However, Glenn insists that, at heart, he is a "rice guy." Unfortunately, the economics of growing heritage rice prove entirely unprofitable. "It's not a business venture, but a cultural venture," says Glenn. Thankfully, the other crops help sustain his efforts.

Glenn's steadfast dedication to quality — demonstrated in such painstaking practices as cold-milling and on-demand production — has garnered him quite a following from the very beginning. Top southern chefs like Anne Quatrono, Louis Osteen, and Frank Stitt bought Glenn's first corn and rice, and others from around the country soon followed suit. Within the first few years Charlie Trotter, Thomas Keller, and Daniel Boulud all recognized the importance of Glenn's vision and the superior product he provided.

However, it must be noted that despite his celebrity chef roster and unequivocal success, Glenn shrugs off any praise. His primary allegiance remains the same – the preservation of heritage seeds. Through Anson Mills and the Carolina Gold Rice Foundation, he seeks to enlist farmers on his mission. Not only does Glenn contract farmers in growing the crops but also in milling the product. He proclaims with pride that even his accountant can operate a combine. Glenn assists in all areas of the process – from the field to the mill to the paperwork. His longtime business ally, Catherine Schopfer, brokers the grains, which basically entails constant communication with their commercial customers. Glenn's wife, Kay, is a free-lance writer who met him when the New York Times sent her down South to capture his story. Now, she attempts to capture his knowledge for use on the Anson Mills website – www.ansonmills.com – which catalogs their various products.

Daring to distill the facts running through Glenn's head should be lauded. Like his ambition, they seem ceaseless. Glenn has a favorite expression when describing folks he really admires – from farmers to geneticists. He will say that they have forgotten more than most of us know. The irony is that he does not realize this statement describes himself perfectly.

Glenn Roberts has definitely forgotten more than most of know, and he's still learning.

* * *

At the GO, we use Anson Mills Carolina Whole Hominy Quick Yellow Grits, Sea Island Red Peas, and Carolina Gold Rice.

CHAPTER 5

Sweets

Sarah's Red Velvet Pound Cake

Mystery surrounds the Red Velvet Cake; the particulars of its origin and ingredients vary from cook to cook. But any bona fide Southerner better have one in their repertoire. Mine comes in the form of a pound cake, as I feel the density stands up beautifully to all that cream cheese frosting! And I certainly don't go light on the food coloring, since red is the point, after all.

Softened butter, for pan
2½ cups sugar
8 large eggs
1 14-ounce can condensed milk
1 tablespoon vanilla extract
2 teaspoons kosher salt
1 pound unsalted butter, melted
2¼ cups cake flour
¾ cup unsweetened cocoa powder, plus more for
    pan
2 teaspoons baking powder
½ cup red food coloring
Cream Cheese Frosting (see recipe below)

Preheat oven to 350 degrees.

Grease a Bundt pan with softened butter and then dust with cocoa powder.

Combine sugar, eggs, condensed milk, vanilla, and salt in a food processor; mix until combined. While running, pour butter into food processor bowl and continue running until thoroughly combined. Pour this mixture into a large mixing bowl. Sift flour, cocoa powder, and baking powder into egg mixture, whisking as you go. Add red food coloring; whisk to combine. Pour batter into pan.

Bake until a toothpick inserted into the center comes out clean, about 1½ hours. Remove from oven and allow to cool for 10 minutes. Release from pan onto serving plate.

Allow to thoroughly cool.

Applying frosting to a cake is a battle against crumbs. It is easier done when the cake is cold since it will be less likely to crumble; thus, there will be several trips back and forth to the refrigerator during the icing process.

To frost: Refrigerate the cake until cold. Once cold, remove the cake and apply a thin layer of Cream Cheese Frosting using an icing spatula. Return cake to refrigerator until frosting hardens. Remove cake and apply remaining frosting using icing spatula. Refrigerate until frosting stiffens up a bit. Slice while cold, but cake is best served at room temperature.

YIELD: 16 to 20 servings

CREAM CHEESE FROSTING
24 ounces cream cheese, softened
15 tablespoons unsalted butter, softened
2¼ cups powdered sugar, sifted
2 tablespoons vanilla extract
2 tablespoons fresh lemon juice

Combine the cream cheese and butter in a large bowl and beat with an electric mixer until smooth and fluffy, 2 to 3 minutes. Add the sugar, vanilla, and lemon juice and mix on low speed until combined.

P.S. The icing can be made in advance and refrigerated but should be brought to room temperature before using.

Gingerbread Pound Cake

With all its warm spices, I can't imagine an aroma more evocative of the holidays than that of gingerbread. The fragrance and flavor truly seem to connect folks with sweet memories that they love to share. One such customer told me of his mother's gingerbread with a lemon glaze, and the contrasting flavors intrigued me so much that I took this suggestion. To me, this is how the best foods come about – by sharing. So, please pass this recipe along and feel free to add your own favorite variations!

Softened butter, for pan
1½ cups packed light brown sugar
1¼ cups dark molasses
¼ cup honey
8 large eggs
1 tablespoon vanilla extract
2 teaspoons kosher salt
1 pound unsalted butter, melted
3 cups cake flour, plus more for pan
2 tablespoons ground cinnamon
2 tablespoons ground ginger
2 tablespoons ground allspice
2 teaspoons baking powder
Lemon Glaze (see recipe below)

Preheat oven to 350 degrees.

Grease a Bundt pan with softened butter and then dust with cake flour.

Combine sugar, molasses, honey, eggs, vanilla, and salt in a food processor. Mix until combined. While running, pour melted butter into food processor bowl and continue running until thoroughly combined. Pour this mixture into a large mixing bowl. Sift flour, cinnamon, ginger, allspice, and baking powder into egg mixture, whisking as you go. Pour batter into prepared pan.

Bake until a toothpick inserted in the center comes out clean, about 1 hour. Remove from oven and allow to cool for 10 minutes. Release from pan onto serving plate. Brush with Lemon Glaze while still warm.

Allow to cool completely before slicing.

YIELD: 16 to 20 servings

P.S. I admit that I do go heavy on the spices (cinnamon, ginger, and allspice) as they are my favorite, and I like a "spicy" gingerbread. However, feel free to cut back these amounts to your personal taste.

P.P.S. Some might find this cake to be a bit heavy at the end of a meal, and I can understand – it has a lot going on! Really, my ideal time to enjoy this cake would be at a special holiday breakfast with a strong cup of coffee.

LEMON GLAZE
½ cup fresh lemon juice
1 cup sugar

Combine ingredients in a small pot and cook over low heat until sugar dissolves and syrup forms. Remove from heat. Brush on cake using a pastry brush.

P.S. The glaze can be made in advance and refrigerated but should be heated before using.

Old Fashioned Butterscotch Pudding

As a child, I LOVED butterscotch pudding. Specifically, I loved the butterscotch pudding that came in the little metal cans! My nostalgia for this memory sent me on a mission to recreate that flavor, but with less industrialized ingredients. Try as I might, most renditions lacked that bit of childhood magic. Thankfully, I found the answer in a bottle of butterscotch schnapps! While this might veer slightly from my all-natural mission, it nails that elusive flavor and makes me feel about 4 years old again.

3 large eggs
2 cups heavy cream
2 cups milk
¼ cup butterscotch schnapps
3 tablespoons vanilla extract
1½ teaspoons kosher salt
1 cup packed light brown sugar
½ cup corn starch

Combine eggs in a medium bowl and gently whisk. Keep near the stovetop as you work on the rest of the recipe.

Combine cream, milk, schnapps, vanilla, and salt in a large pot; set aside. Mix the sugar and corn starch together in a medium bowl. Add a half cup of milk mixture to sugar mixture and whisk to combine. (This is a slurry!)

Heat the milk mixture over medium heat until steaming but not simmering, about 3 minutes. Add the sugar mixture to the milk mixture and cook, stirring constantly, until it begins to thicken. The time for this mixture to thicken may vary as it depends upon the corn starch reaching a certain temperature, but it will be obvious. The mixture will subtly thicken and then quickly become very thick. At this point, it will be at a rolling boil and will pull away from the sides of the pot. Remove pot from the heat.

Slowly drizzle a cup (using a ladle is helpful!) of the hot mixture into the eggs, whisking as you do so. (This is called tempering and should prevent the eggs from scrambling if done very carefully. But do not fret if your egg whites cook just a bit – the mixture will be strained in the final steps, eliminating any unsightly lumps.)

Next, slowly pour the warmed eggs into the hot mixture in the pot, whisking as you do so. Return the pot to the stove over medium heat. Cook, whisking, until the mixture begins to gently boil. Remove from the heat and strain through a chinois or other fine-meshed strainer into a medium bowl. It can be helpful to use a ladle to push the pudding through the chinois. Fill a large bowl with ice water and set the medium bowl of pudding in this larger bowl to chill. As pudding chills, a slight "skin" will form on surface; vigorously whisk to eliminate.

Once cool, cover and refrigerate.

Serve cold with a garnish of whipped cream.

YIELD: 6 to 8 servings; about 6 cups

P.S. Since butterscotch schnapps might not be a staple in your liquor cabinet, it is handy to know that a miniature or "airplane" bottle of schnapps happens to yield ¼ cup (the necessary amount for this recipe)!

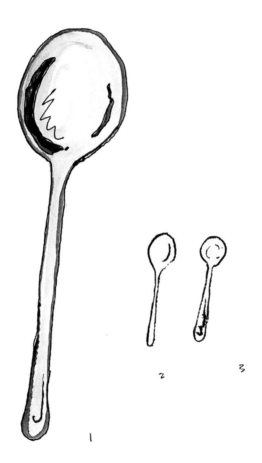

Seasonal Fruit Cobbler

Few desserts are as comforting as cobbler. You might as well be sitting at grandma's house wrapped up in a hand-knit afghan... Seriously, cobbler is that delicious and surprisingly easy to make. Use whatever fruit is in season, such as blackberries or blueberries in the summer, and apples in the fall. If you are using a fruit like apples or peaches, simply peel and slice them into manageable pieces. Serve this straight from the oven with vanilla ice cream, and you are sure to be everyone's best friend.

TOPPING:
1¼ cups self-rising flour
1¼ cups sugar
1 teaspoon kosher salt
8 tablespoons (1 stick) unsalted butter, cut into small pieces, then softened
¾ cup buttermilk

Whisk together the flour, sugar, and salt in a large bowl. Add the butter and work into the dry ingredients, rubbing together with your hands, until the mixture resembles wet sand. Add buttermilk and stir to combine.

FILLING:
Softened butter, for pan
4 cups seasonal fruit, such as berries, apples, or peaches
¼ cup sugar
2 tablespoons honey
1 tablespoon corn starch
Zest and juice of 1 lemon

1 teaspoon cinnamon
1 teaspoon kosher salt
½ teaspoon vanilla extract

Preheat oven to 400 degrees.

Grease a 9-by-13-inch baking dish. Combine all of the filling ingredients in a large bowl; stir to combine. Transfer to baking dish. Top the fruit with large spoonfuls of the batter. (The batter does not need to cover the fruit entirely; it will expand during the baking process.) Bake for about 1 ½ hours, until the top is golden brown and the dough has cooked through. If top becomes too brown and dough still needs to cook more, cover with foil. Serve with vanilla ice cream!

Yield: 8 to 10 servings

World Famous Bread Pudding

At the GO, we have served this dessert since day one, and we have called it "world famous" since day one – it is just that amazing! The secret to its intoxicating powers lies in the beautiful, golden egg yolks that come courtesy of Celeste Albers. Her happy Wadmalaw Island hens lay the best eggs in town, and they are essential to the success of our bread pudding.

Read Celeste's story on page 165.

15 egg yolks
¾ cup plus 3 tablespoons sugar
4½ cups heavy cream
1½ cups milk
2¼ teaspoons vanilla extract
12 cups soft French bread, diced into 1-inch squares
¾ cup chopped pecans
Whiskey Sauce (see recipe below)

Combine egg yolks and sugar in a large bowl; whisk to combine. Add cream, milk, and vanilla; whisk to combine. Add bread and pecans; stir with a wooden spoon until well combined. Cover and refrigerate overnight. (The mixture must be soaked at least overnight and up to a few days in advance.)

Preheat oven to 350 degrees.

Stir mixture well and pour into 9-by-13-inch baking dish. Bake until surface feels firm, 30 to 40 minutes.

Serve warm with Whiskey Sauce. You may pour Whiskey Sauce over pan of bread pudding or pass around in a dish for guests to pour over their individual servings.

YIELD: 8 to 10 servings

WHISKEY SAUCE
1 cup milk
½ cup sugar
2 egg yolks
¼ cup bourbon

Combine egg yolks in a medium bowl and have near stove with a ladle for tempering. Combine milk and sugar in a medium pot over medium heat. Heat milk-sugar mixture until steaming. Ladle a ½ cup of milk-sugar mixture into bowl with egg yolks. Whisk to combine. Add egg mixture to pot with milk-sugar mixture and whisk to combine. Heat until the mixture just begins to simmer.

Remove from heat and pour through a chinois or other fine-meshed strainer into a medium bowl. Fill a large bowl with ice water and set the medium bowl of sauce in this larger bowl to chill. Add bourbon; stir to combine. Cover and refrigerate until ready to use. This can be made several days in advance but should be brought to room temperature before serving.

YIELD: About 1½ cups

Pie/Tart Dough

Even if you happen to be intimidated by pie dough, please do not skip this recipe. I am here to assuage your fears and give some realistic advice. First, the actual making of the dough happens to be relatively easy with the help of the trusty food processor. Second, achieving the end result of a beautiful, golden brown pie crust to fill with your favorite ingredients relies on nothing more complicated than freezing your formed crust in its pan, which protects against shrinkage during the blind baking process. Forming the pie crust is the last step in this recipe, and then you will be ready to move on to our specific pie and tart recipes. Finally, if your first batch of dough does not come out to your liking, please try again. There are subtle nuances to knowing when your dough has reached that perfect consistency, and over time, you will become an expert.

1 pound butter, cut into pea size pieces
4 cups all-purpose flour
2 teaspoons sugar
2 teaspoons salt
½ cup cold water

Freeze butter for 30 minutes. Combine flour, sugar, and salt in the bowl of a food processor and run until combined. Gradually add cold butter (while running) until the mixture resembles wet sand. Gradually, add water (while running) until the mixture balls together. (Your dough may require more or less water – so it is important to add gradually.) Remove dough from food processor. At this point, it should be holding together nicely, but you might need to knead it with your hands to form a solid ball. Divide ball into 3 equal pieces if making dough for pies; divide into 2 equal pieces if making dough for tarts.

Wrap balls in plastic wrap and flatten to form an approximately 4-inch-wide disk. Refrigerate for at least 30 minutes before using. Dough can be made in advance and refrigerated for up to one week, or frozen up to one month. Simply allow to come to a pliable temperature before using.

Once ready to use, roll out your dough, using a rolling pin, on a lightly floured surface. Roll with light pressure from the center out. Combat moderate sticking by dusting liberally with flour. If dough seems excessively sticky, it is probably too warm and should be returned to the refrigerator for another 15 minutes. (You can drape it over the back of a pie plate if you need to put it back in the refrigerator.)

Continue to roll out the dough, dusting with more flour as necessary. Stop several times to turn dough (as if winding a clock) so that all sides receive equal attention. You might also flip dough over, or at least dust other side, to make sure there is no sticking on the backside! When dough is about ¼ inch thick, place pie or tart pan on top to check for accurate size. Your disk of dough should be about 10 inches in diameter.

To transfer the dough from the table to your pan, simply fold it in half and then in half again so that you have a triangular piece. Place this in your pan with the pointy end at the center of the pan. Unfold and press into pan. At this point, there are slightly different techniques depending on your goal of pie or tart.

To finish your pie: Press dough firmly into the bottom and sides of the pan. Some crust should be hanging over edges of pan; trim with scissors so that only about ¼ inch hangs over. Using a fork, press dough into rim of pan; this technique is decorative but also helps to prevent shrinkage during baking. Wrap again in plastic and freeze crust for at least one hour – but up to one week – in advance.

To finish your tart: Press dough firmly into the bottom and fluted sides of the tart pan. There should be a good amount hanging over edges. Trim with scissors or simply roll your rolling pin over the top of the pan. The sharp edge of the pan should trim dough neatly.

This next step is an extra precaution I have invented to deal with shrinkage of crust during baking. Take excess dough (that you just trimmed from outer edges) and roll out onto floured surface until about ¼ inch thick. Cut dough into strips that are about ¾ inch in width. Press these strips into dough that is embedded in fluted edges of pan. Line the entire edge of pan with this "reinforcement." The dough should be pliable enough to stick together, and the two pieces will ultimately form one piece during baking. Discard any remaining dough. Wrap and freeze crust for at least one hour – but up to one week – in advance.

Yield: 3 9-inch pie crusts or 2 9½-inch tart crusts

P.S. From here you can move on to any pie/tart recipe. I do blind bake all of my crusts, meaning that I
bake them (with pie weights) until golden brown before adding any sort of filling (even if further baking is
required after filling). I include this process in all of our
pie/tart recipes.

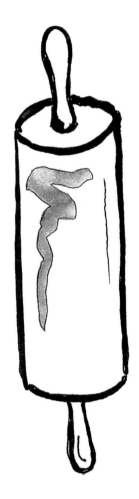

Chocolate Pecan Tart

This is my take on a classic Southern recipe – Kentucky Derby Pie – which has gained fame far beyond its home state. Reading the ingredients, you will quickly understand its popularity. What's not to like? Pecans, chocolate, and bourbon make this a hit at any gathering!

1 unbaked frozen tart shell (see recipe on page 139)
8 cups uncooked rice or dried beans, for use as pie weights
1½ cups pecan pieces
1 cup semisweet chocolate chips
3 large eggs, beaten
1 cup light corn syrup
½ cup packed light brown sugar
½ cup heavy cream
2 tablespoons unsalted butter, melted
1 tablespoon bourbon
1 teaspoon kosher salt
1 teaspoon vanilla extract

Preheat oven to 350 degrees.

Line tart shell with a sheet of tinfoil. Spread rice or beans across the tart shell, mounding them up a bit on the sides and going more lightly in the center.

Place tart shell on baking sheet. Bake until edges are dark golden brown and center has just begun to golden, about 1 hour.

Remove from oven and allow to cool with tinfoil and weights still in place. Once cool, remove weights and reserve the weights for another day.

Spread the pecans and chocolate chips evenly across the bottom of the tart shell.

In a small pot, whisk the remaining ingredients together over medium heat. Cook until hot but not simmering. Pour the filling over the pecans and chocolate chips, but be sure not to overfill. Since crust will shrink to varying degrees, you might have a touch more filling than you can safely fit in your crust. Simply discard extra filling.

Bake until the filling sets and puffs up slightly, about 30 minutes. Remove from the oven and allow to cool completely before slicing. (I prefer allowing my tart to cool and then refrigerating until completely chilled, which makes for easy slicing.)

Serve at room temperature with whipped cream or vanilla ice cream.

YIELD: 8 servings

P.S. The tart can be made in advance and refrigerated but should be brought to room temperature before serving.

P.P.S. This recipe will also work for a pie pan, but you might need to cut back just a bit on pecans and chocolate chips. And you will most likely have some extra filling. I simply think it is more impressive as a tart, but there is no reason to run out and buy another pan!

Ruth's Key Lime Pie

Full credit for this pie goes to Ruth Penn of Jacksonville, Florida – an amazing cook and friend. I changed only her meringue to a very stable version that I prefer in a restaurant setting. Otherwise, this is the same pie I have eaten every summer of my life, made exclusively by Ruth!

Read Ruth's story on page 161.

1 unbaked frozen pie shell (see recipe on page 139)
6 cups uncooked rice or dried beans, for use as pie
    weights
4 large eggs
1 14-ounce can condensed milk
½ cup Joe and Nell's Key lime juice (Ruth prefers this
    brand!)
Meringue (see recipe below)

Preheat oven to 350 degrees.

Line pie shell with a sheet of tinfoil. Spread rice or beans across the pie shell, mounding them up a bit on the sides and going more lightly in the center.

Place pie shell on baking sheet. Bake until edges are dark golden brown and center has just begun to golden. Check crust's progress at 30 minutes, but total baking time should be about 45 minutes.

Remove from oven and allow to cool with tinfoil and weights still in place. Once cool, remove weights and reserve the weights for another day. Discard tinfoil. Reserve crust until filling and meringue are both made. The crust can be baked off one day in advance, wrapped, and held at room temperature.

To make filling, separate the eggs – put yolks into a medium bowl, one white into a small bowl, and the remaining 3 whites into another small bowl to reserve for meringue. Add condensed milk and key lime juice to bowl of yolks; whisk to combine. Beat one egg white until frothy and fold into the bowl of yolks. Reserve filling until meringue is made.

Once meringue is made, pour filling into prebaked crust. Dollop the meringue on top of the filling using a rubber spatula, making sure meringue reaches edges of pie to form a seal; this will help with meringue's shrinkage during baking. Bake until the meringue turns golden brown, about 30 minutes.

Allow pie to cool to room temperature, then transfer to refrigerator for complete cooling, about 6 hours. Pie is best served the day it is made. It can be held overnight, but doing so will compromise the quality of the meringue.

To serve, dip a knife in hot water, wipe dry, and slice in half. Repeat process, then slice into quarters. Repeat process, then slice into eighths.

YIELD: 8 servings

P.S. The meringue will "weep" some during/after baking. This is due to moisture in the egg whites and really should not pose a problem nor be too excessive, thanks to this very stable meringue recipe.

MERINGUE
6 egg whites
1 teaspoon cream of tartar
¾ cup of sugar
¹/₃ cup water
1 tablespoon cornstarch
1 teaspoon vanilla extract

Combine egg whites in a large bowl. Beat with an electric mixer until foamy. Add cream of tartar; beat until body begins to build. Gradually add sugar; beat until moderately stiff peaks form; reserve.

Combine water, cornstarch, vanilla, and salt in a small pot or skillet. Cook over medium heat, stirring, until gel forms, about 30 seconds. Remove from heat.

Spoon cornstarch mixture into egg white mixture; beat to combine. At this point, your meringue should be stable and shiny.

YIELD: Meringue for 1 pie (Double this recipe for a tart!)

P.S. Meringue can be a bear in a restaurant setting, as it does not want to hold up well. Here, the use of cornstarch creates a more stable meringue, a trick I learned from the wonderful cookbooks of Shirley Corriher.

P.P.S. Do not be surprised at the amount of meringue produced by this recipe; it is indeed substantial. But I find that folks who love meringue pies really want a little pie and a lot of meringue!

Lisa's Coconut Cream Pie

I met my good friend Lisa Maki first as a customer at the GO. She had a neighboring startup business, and they basically thought of us as their personal corporate cafeteria. At the time, I had no idea what a talented cook Lisa happened to be, but many Sunday suppers later, I felt just as enamored of her food as she did of ours. And I coveted her Coconut Cream Pie recipe! She claims that a west coast restaurant inspired hers, but I think it totally belongs to Lisa. I've only restaurantified it slightly – using my go-to custard technique, as I know it's foolproof.

1 unbaked frozen pie shell (see recipe on page 139)
2 large eggs
1 13½-ounce can unsweetened coconut milk
1½ cups heavy cream
1 teaspoon vanilla extract
1 teaspoon kosher salt
¾ cup sugar
¹/₃ cup cornstarch
1½ cups flaked coconut, toasted
Whipped Cream, for garnish (see recipe below)

Preheat oven to 350 degrees.

Line pie shell with a sheet of tinfoil. Spread rice or beans across the pie shell, mounding them up a bit on the sides and going more lightly in the center.

Place pie shell on baking sheet. Bake until edges are dark golden brown and center has just begun to golden. Check crust's progress at 30 minutes, but total baking time should be about 45 minutes. Remove from oven and allow to cool with tinfoil and weights still in place. Once cool, remove weights and reserve the weights for another day. Reserve crust until filling is made. The crust can be baked off one day in advance, wrapped, and held at room temperature.

To make filling, combine eggs in a medium bowl and gently whisk. Keep near the stovetop as you work on the rest of the recipe.

Combine coconut milk, cream, vanilla, and salt in a large pot. Mix the sugar and corn starch together in a medium bowl. Add a half cup of coconut milk mixture to sugar mixture and whisk to combine. (This is a slurry!)

Heat the coconut milk mixture over medium heat until steaming but not simmering. Add the sugar mix-ture to the coconut milk mixture and cook, stirring constantly, until it begins to thicken. The time for this mixture to thicken may vary as it depends upon the corn starch reaching a certain temperature, but it will be obvious. The mixture will subtly thicken and then quickly become very thick. At this point it will be at a rolling boil and will pull away from sides of the pot. Remove pot from the heat.

Slowly drizzle a cup (using a ladle is helpful!) of the hot mixture into the eggs, whisking as you do so. (This is called tempering and should prevent the eggs from scrambling if done very carefully. But do not fret if your egg whites cook just a bit – the mixture will be strained in the final steps, eliminating any unsightly lumps.)

Next, slowly pour the warmed eggs into the hot mixture in the pot, whisking as you do so. Return the pot to the stove over medium heat. Cook, whisking, until the mixture begins to gently boil. Remove from the heat and strain through a chinois or other fine-meshed strainer into a medium bowl. It can be helpful to use a ladle to push the custard through the chinois. Fill a large bowl with ice water and set the medium bowl of custard in this larger bowl to chill. As custard chills a slight "skin" will form on surface; vigorously whisk to eliminate. Once cool, stir in 1 cup of toasted coconut.

Spoon custard into reserved pie crust, spreading with a rubber spatula to evenly distribute. Cover and refrigerate for at least a few hours or overnight. (This will ensure that the custard fully sets, and the pie is easy to slice.)

Remove from refrigerator when ready to serve. Cover entire pie with Whipped Cream (see recipe below) and garnish with remaining ½ cup of toasted coconut.

YIELD: 8 servings

P.S. Lisa covers the pie with whipped cream before slicing (as described above), but if you will not be serving the entire pie in one serving, you can simply garnish each slice individually with whipped cream and toasted coconut.

WHIPPED CREAM
1 cup heavy cream
2 tablespoons powdered sugar
1 tablespoon vanilla extract

Whip cream until soft peaks form, using a whisk or electric mixer. Sift in powdered sugar, add vanilla, and continue whipping until moderately stiff peaks form.

Chocolate Chip Cookies

I consider these a pretty classic rendition of every-one's childhood favorite treat. I do insist on light brown sugar to make them extra moist and delicious.

1½ cups packed light brown sugar
½ pound (2 sticks) unsalted butter, softened
1 teaspoon vanilla extract
1 teaspoon kosher salt
2 large eggs
2¼ cups all-purpose flour
1 teaspoon baking powder
½ teaspoon baking soda
1½ cups semi-sweet chocolate chips

Preheat oven to 350 degrees.

Combine the sugar, butter, vanilla, and salt in a large bowl. Beat with an electric mixer on high speed, until color becomes lighter and mixture is somewhat fluffy, about 2 minutes. Scrape down the sides of the bowl with a rubber spatula. Add the eggs; beat until well combined. Scrape down the sides of the bowl with a rubber spatula and sift the flour, baking powder, and baking soda into the wet mixture in increments, beating on low speed between each addition, until dough comes together. Fold in chocolate chips with a rubber spatula.

Using a tablespoon, scoop about 2 spoonfuls of the dough into a ball and place on a non-stick baking sheet (or line sheet with wax or parchment paper). Repeat with remaining dough, keeping the scoops about 2 inches apart. Using your fingers or the back of the spoon, press down on each ball of dough to slightly flatten. You should get about 9 cookies on each sheet.

Bake until golden brown, about 15 minutes. (Depending on the size of your oven, you may need to do this in batches.)

Remove the cookies from the oven and allow to cool. Repeat with the remaining sheets, if necessary.

YIELD: About 2 dozen cookies

Oatmeal Raisin Cookies

The best thing about oatmeal cookies is that they almost seem healthy – like a granola bar, right? I make mine with plenty of cinnamon and allspice, as it seems to supplement my delusion!

2 cups packed light brown sugar
½ pound (2 sticks) unsalted butter, softened
2 teaspoons vanilla extract
2 teaspoons kosher salt
4 large eggs
2½ cups all-purpose flour
2 teaspoons cinnamon
1 teaspoon allspice
1 teaspoon baking powder
1 teaspoon baking soda
3 cups oats
2 cups raisins

Preheat oven to 350 degrees.

Combine the sugar, butter, vanilla, and salt in a large bowl. Beat with an electric mixer on high speed, until color becomes lighter and mixture is somewhat fluffy, about 2 minutes. Scrape down the sides of the bowl with a rubber spatula. Add the eggs; beat until well combined. Scrape down the sides of the bowl with a rubber spatula and sift the flour, cinnamon, allspice, baking powder, and baking soda into the wet mixture in increments, beating on low speed between each addition, until dough comes together. Add oats and beat on low speed until well combined. Fold in raisins with a rubber spatula.

Using a tablespoon, scoop about 2 spoonfuls of the dough into a ball and place on a non-stick baking sheet (or line sheet with wax or parchment paper). Repeat with remaining dough, keeping the scoops about 2 inches apart. Using your fingers or the back of the spoon, press down on each ball of dough to slightly flatten. You should get about 9 cookies on each sheet.

Bake until golden brown, about 15 minutes. (Depending on the size of your oven, you may need to do this in batches.)

Remove the cookies from the oven and allow to cool. Repeat with the remaining sheets, if necessary.

YIELD: About 2 dozen cookies

Peanut Butter & Chocolate Cookies

I have to admit that a customer convinced me that peanut butter cookies really are better with chocolate chips. I know the same argument could be made for just about any cookie, but the pairing of peanut butter and chocolate seems too ridiculously good to deny. And so I acquiesce – peanut butter and chocolate forever!

2 cups packed light brown sugar
½ pound (2 sticks) unsalted butter, softened
1 cup extra crunchy peanut butter
1 teaspoon vanilla extract
1 teaspoon kosher salt
2½ cups all-purpose flour
1 teaspoon baking powder
½ teaspoon baking soda
3 large eggs
1½ cups semi-sweet chocolate chips

Preheat oven to 350 degrees.

Combine the sugar, butter, peanut butter, vanilla, and salt in a large bowl. Beat with an electric mixer on high speed, until color becomes lighter and mixture is somewhat fluffy, about 2 minutes. Scrape down the sides of the bowl with a rubber spatula. Add the eggs; beat until well combined. Scrape down the sides of the bowl with a rubber spatula and sift the flour, baking powder, and baking soda into the wet mixture in increments, beating on low speed between each addition, until dough comes together. Fold in chocolate chips with a rubber spatula.

Using a tablespoon, scoop about 2 spoonfuls of the dough into a ball and place on a non-stick baking sheet (or line sheet with wax or parchment paper). Repeat with remaining dough, keeping the scoops about 2 inches apart. Using your fingers or the back of the spoon, press down on each ball of dough to slightly flatten. You should get about 9 cookies on each sheet.

Bake until golden brown, about 15 minutes. (Depending on the size of your oven, you may need to do this in batches.)

Remove the cookies from the oven and allow to cool. Repeat with the remaining sheets, if necessary.

YIELD: About 2 dozen cookies

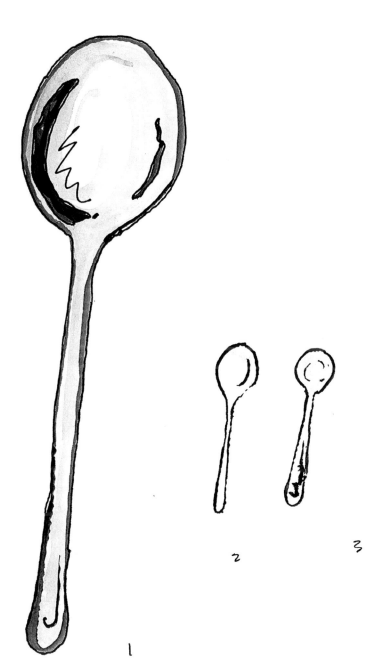

1

2

3

Sarah O'Kelley with Ruth Penn

Ruth Penn – The Queen of Key Lime Pie

If one dessert defined my childhood, it was Ruth's Key Lime Pie. With a tangy, creamy center and billowing, ethereal meringue, it was quite simply heaven.

Every summer I awaited our family trips to Jacksonville, Florida with the anticipation most children reserve for Christmas. I craved the ocean and the sand, but mostly I yearned for Ruth. To me, she embodied every familial female figure. She would hug and commiserate and champion me throughout my life, and most of this happened inside the sturdy, old walls of our beach house kitchen.

Ruth Penn began cooking for my grandmother and her sister in the summer of 1973 (or thereabouts). During the rest of the year, she worked for the Duval County Public School System cooking in schools around the city.

"I loved it. It was my passion," she says. "Feeding other people; watching them eat."

At home, Ruth had her own nine children to feed, and really, that was her initial impetus for cooking. Ironically, as a child herself, growing up in Annapolis, Maryland, Ruth Lililan Johnson had little interest in the kitchen.

"I was an outside person," she says. "I liked to be gone!"

However, good cooking surrounded Ruth – this she could not escape. Her father loved food and cooked everything from local vegetables to leg of lamb. And her grandmother ran a small baking business from her home kitchen. Ruth and her siblings spent a few days every week at her house – watching and helping with pound cakes, cobblers, and her famous dinner rolls.

When Ruth married James Penn Jr. (known affectionately as "Penn"), she moved to a naval base in Portsmouth, Virginia. It was there that she remembers cooking her first big meal. Penn's family made the trip up from North Carolina, bringing a ham and such; but she had to prepare the greens, which she knew nothing about. Penn guided her through the cleaning of the greens, and then Ruth just threw them in a pot with water and a piece of meat. Ruth laughs now, remembering the family arriving to greens floating in a pot of water.

"Girl, you don't know how to cook greens!" they said. Then they took the greens out of the water and started over.

But over the years, Ruth taught herself the ways of the kitchen through trial and error – cooking everything from spaghetti to fried chicken, and finally Key lime pie.

She remembers that in the early 80s my grandmother came to the beach after a trip to Key West raving about this pie. She even brought Ruth a postcard with the recipe on it. Ruth had never heard of it, but just followed the instructions on that card, and that's what she has been doing every summer since.

Ruth believes that the trick to the pie is in the meringue. "You have to make sure it's whipped to a certain level and browned to perfection," she says. And I agree.

But I also believe the true secret lies in Ruth and the love she imparts with every bite.

Celeste Albers

Celeste Albers

The Woman Behind the Golden Eggs

Celeste Albers is an iconic figure in the Lowcountry farming community. Her Sea Island Eggs are coveted by Charleston restaurants, and at the GO, we are lucky to serve them.

Cracking one open reveals a yolk as golden as a sunset. They literally *make* our bearnaise, deviled eggs, and desserts. During the heat of summer when the hens simply refuse to lay enough, we enter a time of mourning. We substitute other high-quality, farm-fresh eggs, but the bearnaise turns a pale yellow, more reminiscent of the washed-out midday sun than its evening splendor.

So who is the woman behind the golden eggs? Celeste's roots lie in the Lowcountry. Her grandfather shrimped in Bulls Bay and ran a country store on Highway 17 near Awendaw. However, her father left farming to earn an accounting degree and wound up working for DuPont in Delaware. She remembers that he hated his job, and he eventually ended up back in Awendaw, farming the family land.

In 1993, Celeste moved down with her baby daughter, Erin, and joined him. She began selling their produce at the fledgling Charleston Farmers Market. There she met George Albers, who was selling his own produce. Celeste remembers that George used to stop by her booth, buy some of her wild blackberries, and chat for a while.

"It was the blackberries that did it," says Celeste. "George stole me away from my dad, and before you knew it we had one booth instead of two."

Together, they have navigated the rough terrain of making a living off the land. They have grown vegetables, shrimped, and finally raised chickens and cows. None of it has proven easy, especially since they lease rather than own their property – negating any meager security you might expect a farmer to have. Furthermore, they physically labor every day of the year.

But Celeste maintains that she would rather this than a lifetime of working a job she hates. These days they do seem to have found their niche: focusing on their egg and raw milk production. And among those in the know, their product has achieved a cult-like following.

At the GO, we regularly receive phone calls from avid Celeste fans wanting to reserve their eggs and milk, and I truly understand their reverence. When the eggs become scarce, I reserve them for use only in our bread pudding, and with each of the 40 eggs I crack, I give thanks to Celeste.

Chris Stewart